500 Really Useful English Phrases

From Intermediate to Fluency

Jenny Smith.

©Fluency Today 2014

Please visit my website and join my newsletter for free study materials and information about my other books.

www.englishfluencytoday.com

All rights reserved. No part of this book can be reproduced or distributed in any form whatsoever without the permission of the publisher. The only exceptions are short quotations and some non-commercial uses allowed by copyright laws.

All efforts have been made to make the contents as accurate as possible. However if there are inaccuracies the publisher cannot be held liable. This book contains short stories and example sentences, all of which are fictitious and not based on any real event or person.

Table of Contents.

Do you feel 'stuck' in the intermediate level?	4
The New Business	6
The Summer Holiday	14
The Bully	20
The Divorce and The Marriage	26
The Fashion Show	32
The End and then the Beginning	38
The Birthday Party	44
School Days	47
Boy Hears Girl	51
The Dead End Job?	57
Fake	65
A Tale of Three Careers	72
The Art of Negotiation	78
Does Ambition Equal Happiness?	81
The Time Travel Record Shop	86
Teenage Runaways	92
Never a Lender or Borrower Be	98
Reality TV! Reality?	103
Spread Betting	110
The Secret? The Lie?	116
The Personality Makeover	122
Unrequited Love	128
Do Children Still Play Outside?	132

Jargon Buster	138
Death of the Job. Birth of Opportunity	144
The Wind up Merchant	150
Internet Dating	161
The Family Holiday	172
Goodbye	180

Do you feel 'stuck' in the intermediate level?

I started writing this book because I could see that once students had studied all of the basic grammar and vocabulary and could communicate to a fairly good level they just sort of got stuck there and never really improved very much.

The problem was that they really needed to start using and being exposed to **real English** that is in everyday use. However, the usual textbooks just sort of continue teaching the same boring stuff and don't take into account that the students need to be challenged by using 'real' English and not just lists of grammar.

Of course the student could just pick up an English language newspaper or watch TV but that could be a bit off-putting or intimidating if they had no guidance as to how to use the new language being introduced. This is where this book fits in; it bridges the gap between being comfortable with beginner and lower intermediate grammar/vocabulary and being able to comfortably use normal English language books, magazines, television etc.

This series uses interesting stories to help the student learn everyday English naturally and in a fun and engaging way. It also features easy to understand explanations and example sentences to ensure the student is guided from the intermediate to the advanced level without ever feeling confused or lost.

How does this book help you move from intermediate to advanced English?

Reason 1. It will help you understand everyday English by introducing 500 commonly used phrases. It also features both descriptions and examples so students can fully understand the meaning of the phrases.

Reason 2. It makes learning fun and interesting. All of the phrases are used in context in interesting short stories and articles. You can see how the phrases are actually used in everyday life.

Reason 3. It uses easy to understand English to introduce more difficult phrases. So you can improve smoothly.

Reason 4. One of the things about being an advanced speaker is that you can speak fluently on any subject. The stories are all about particular subjects and feature the phrases you will need to speak fluently on that subject.

This book is written for people who have reached the intermediate level but are finding it difficult to move forward. By studying phrases in context in a fun and interesting way you will be improving naturally and be learning English that people actually use rather than just 'classroom English'. You will actually start to sound like a native English speaker.

So let's get started and move from the intermediate to the advanced level.

The New Business

Part One

Years ago when I was still in my twenties and still working for a large company I decided to throw caution to the wind and start my own business. At the beginning it was by no means plain sailing and I had to get through a lot of bad times. At one point I had a close shave with bankruptcy but I was able to get a big sale just in the nick of time and my company was saved.

Phrases:

Throw caution to the wind: to take a risk.
Example: *Even though he doesn't have much experience, let's throw caution to the wind and hire him.*

By no means: this means 'definitely not'.
Example: *Of course you can run a marathon, but by no means is it going to be easy.*

Plain Sailing: this is used when you want to say that something is easy and that the process was smooth.
Example: *I studied very hard so the exams were basically plain sailing.*

A close shave: a lucky escape from danger.
Example: *That was a close shave. He almost caught me reading his private diary.*

In the nick of time: just in time.
Example: *I got paid just in the nick of time. I'd just run out of money.*

Part Two

At one point I totally ran out of money and had to let go of a few staff members. This rough patch lasted for the best part of a year but I was able to ride it out and keep my company running long enough until business improved. In retrospect, while this was a difficult period for me, the upshot was that I was able to pick up a lot of new skills and became much more self-reliant.

Phrases:

To run out of (something): to use up all of your supplies of something.
Example: *We are about to run out of petrol/gas, so let's stop at the next station.*

To let go of staff: this is a nice way of saying 'the staff member was fired or made redundant'. It is often used when it is not the employee's fault, when the company can't afford to employ them any longer etc.
Example: *Because of the recession we have had to let half of our staff go.*

Rough Patch: this means 'a difficult period of time'.
Example: After I lost my job I went through a rough patch financially.

For the best part of a (time period): this is used to express the fact that something lasted for most of a certain time period.
Example 1: *I was ill for the best part of last month.*
Example 2: *I'll be in Indonesia for the best part of next year.*

To ride it out: to endure a bad situation.

Example: *I have no choice but to ride it out and wait for the economy to recover.*

In retrospect: this is used when looking back at a situation/incident. It has the feeling that you would do things differently than you did in the past.
Example 1: *In retrospect, I could have handled that better.*
Example 2: *In retrospect, I should have saved some money when I was younger.*

The upshot is..: this is used when you want to say that there is a positive point to a (sometimes) negative situation.
Example: *My job went from full-time to part-time so I have less money, but the upshot is that I now get to spend more time with my family.*

To pick (something) up: here we mean to gain or learn a new skill.
Example: *He picks up languages very quickly.*

PART THREE

Although I did <u>go out on a limb</u> when I started my company and I had to endure some hard times (at one time it just felt like <u>one thing after another</u>), business eventually <u>took a turn for the better</u>. It's difficult <u>to put my finger on</u> when things <u>started to look up</u> but I think it was when I hired a new manager. She is absolutely amazing and in my eyes she <u>can do no wrong</u>.

<u>Phrases:</u>

To go out on a limb: to take a risk.
Example: *Even though you don't have that much experience, I'm going to go out on a limb and hire you.*

One thing after another: this phrase is used when lots of negative incidents happen in a short space of time.
Example: *First I lost my wallet and then my car was stolen. It's been one thing after another recently.*

Note: <u>If it's not one thing it's another:</u> this is another phrase similar to the one above expressing the feeling that there have been lots of problems. This is often used about people.
Example: *If it's not one thing it's another with that guy. He's just never happy with anything.*

To take a turn for the worse/better: this means when a situation changes for the better/worse.
Example: *His health has really taken a turn for the worse.*

To put one's finger on something: to identify what the issue is, or to pinpoint the core of an issue.

Example: *I can't put my finger on it but I just don't trust him for some reason.*

Things are looking up: this is used when you think that a situation is getting better or improving.
Example: *Now that the economy is beginning to recover, things are really looking up for my company.*

She/he can do no wrong: this means that 'in my opinion this person is perfect'.
Example: *I love that author; she can do no wrong in my opinion.*

PART FOUR

I think that when you are responsible for everything and you are losing money it's very easy to <u>blow things out of proportion</u> and get angry and frustrated about everything. The problem with that is, that it's a <u>vicious circle</u> because the angrier you get the worse you concentrate and the worse you concentrate the worse your business gets. Once I realised what the problem was I was able to <u>turn things around</u> <u>in no time</u>. My advice to people experiencing problems with their business is that <u>no matter what</u> happens don't <u>put off</u> dealing with problems, as they will grow and grow. You may <u>get away with</u> ignoring things for a while but in the end <u>it will dawn on you</u> that <u>there's no time like the present</u> to deal with problems.

Phrases:

To blow (something) out of proportion: to act or believe that something is more serious than it really is (this phrase is used in a negative way).
Example: *I was only 5 minutes late but my boss is acting like I've just bankrupted the company. He's always blowing things out of proportion.*

Vicious Circle: this describes a bad situation that you can't get out of. For example: you have no money because you can't get a job> you can't get job because you can't afford the training> you can't afford training because you have no money etc etc.
Example: *If I work all the time I'm never at home and never see my family but if I take time off we won't have enough money to survive. It's a vicious circle.*

To turn things around: this means to work hard and change a bad situation into a good one.

Example: *When he joined the company it was almost bankrupt, but he worked day and night and turned the company around so it is now very successful.*

In no time: This means very quickly.
Example: Don't worry about moving to a new school, you are very popular and you'll make new friends in no time.

No matter what……: regardless of...
Example: *No matter what you say, I'm not going to let you go.*

To put something off: to delay doing something.
Example: *I hate going there, so I keep putting it off.*

To get away with (something): to not get caught/punished for doing something wrong.
Example: *My teacher didn't notice that I didn't come to class, so I think that I got away with it.*
Note: the phrase 'he/she got away with murder' means that they did not get punished or reprimanded for doing something very wrong.

It dawned on me that….: to realise something.
Example: *It dawned on me that we are too busy, so we need to employ some new staff.*

There's no time like the present: if you are going to do something you should do it now, not wait for some future time.
Example: *I always wanted to go to Jamaica, then this morning I decided that there's no time like the present so I booked my ticket and I leave next week.*

The Summer Holiday

Part One

When I was 19 years old I won a free holiday to France. I was <u>over the moon</u> and wanted to bring my best friend with me. Unfortunately my parents insisted that I bring my younger brother so in the end <u>I had no choice but to</u> go with him. I love my brother but he is very forgetful and never <u>thinks things through</u> so we were <u>bound to</u> get into trouble. Anyway, it was the morning that we were meant to leave and <u>as per usual</u> my brother was running late so I completely <u>flew off the handle</u>. We had a big argument but eventually my brother <u>backed down</u> and we <u>made up</u> and then set off on our trip.

Phrases:

To be over the moon: to be very happy.
Example: *I was over the moon when I got my exam results.*

No choice but to…this is used to indicate that there is only one option (usually this is used when you don't like that option).
Example: *When I broke my leg, I had no choice but to cut my trip short and return home.*

To think (something) through: to think about something in detail and from all angles.
Example: *I don't think that he's thought this through. He seems to think that marriage is the same as just dating someone.*

Bound to: this means that something is inevitable/that of course it happened/will happen.
Example: *if you drink and drive, you are bound to have an accident.*

As per usual: this means that what you are describing is unsurprising because it often happens.
Example: *My bus was late this morning as per usual, so my boss got angry with me.*

To fly off the handle: to suddenly get overly angry
Example: *I always feel like I have to be careful with her as she has a tendency to fly off the handle over the smallest thing.*

To back down: This is when you concede, or when you stop defending your position.
Example: *Her husband backs down too easily and she always gets her own way.*

To make up with (someone): when you have a fight/argument with someone and make peace/ become friends again with them afterwards.
Example: *We do argue sometimes but we always make up afterwards.*

Part Two

When we arrived at the airport the man at the counter said that we had missed our flight. I couldn't believe my ears and as far as I was concerned it was all my brother's fault. I'm not one to hold a grudge so I soon forgave him and we tried to work out how we could still make it to France. We decided that the first thing we should do is go to the bar and let off a little steam. After a while we got talking to the bar man and he suggested that we explain our situation to the airline and see if they would put us on a later flight. We decided to give it a go and luckily we were able to catch a later flight.

Phrases:

I couldn't believe my eyes/ears: used when what you are seeing/hearing is unbelievable.
Example: *I couldn't believe my eyes when he finally stood up to that bully.*

As far as I'm concerned: in my opinion/as much as the situation affects me (often used about personal situations).
Example: *As far as I'm concerned that matter is over.*

(I'm) not one to…: this is used to mean that (I) don't usually (do something).
Example: *I'm not one to worry, but this situation has got me a little concerned.*

To hold a grudge: to keep resenting someone/something.
Example: *Usually I'm not one to hold a grudge, but I just can't forgive him for what he did.*

To work out how to (do something): to discover or think of the method for doing something.
Example: *I could never work out how to iron a shirt properly.*

To make it to (somewhere): to reach, or try to reach a destination. This has the feeling that for some reason it is difficult to get to the destination.
Example: *even though I missed my train I still made it to work on time.*

To let off steam: this is used when you use an activity (like drinking alcohol) to get rid of stress.
Example: *I heard that lots of Japanese people go to karaoke to let off steam.*

To give (something) a go: to try something new.
Example: *I don't usually like team sports but I'll give it a go.*

Part Three

When we arrived in France we <u>came across</u> an excellent café and <u>went</u> completely <u>overboard</u> eating all of the delicious French food. Then suddenly we realised that we had left our wallets in the bar in England! We were completely panicked and went through our bags to <u>make sure</u> we hadn't misplaced our money. We thought for a second about <u>making a run for it</u> but that is illegal, <u>not to mention</u> immoral. In the end we <u>came clean</u> with the café owner and explained our situation. The owner thought it was very funny and offered to let us stay with his family while we sorted out our money situation. It <u>turned out</u> to be one of the best holidays of my life. I think <u>once in a while</u> bad situations end up bringing good luck.

Phrases:

To come across (something/someone): to find something/someone (usually by chance).
Example: *I came across this article about my old school when I was reading the paper this morning.*

To go overboard: to do too much of something. For example if you go overboard with drinking, this means that you drank too much.
Example: *I always go overboard at Christmas and spend too much money on presents.*

To make sure: this means to check that something is correct/ok or in the condition/place that you thought it would be.
Example: *I rang my friend after he got out of hospital, to make sure that he was ok.*

Make a run for it: to try to escape.

Example: *The prisoner saw that the door was open so he tried to make a run for it.*

Not to mention: this is used when you are listing things and then mention something which is obviously important.
Example: *This hotel is the best one I think, it's close to the beach, clean, modern and not to mention it's quite cheap.*

To come clean (about something): this is when you admit to something.
Example: *My son insisted that he didn't break the window but he felt so guilty that he eventually came clean and admitted it.*

To turn out...: was eventually....
Example: *Even though it was raining this morning it turned out to be quite a warm sunny day.*

Once in a while: this means occasionally.
Example: *Once in a while, I like to go to the beach and swim in the sea.*

THE BULLY

PART ONE

Recently I visited the area where I was brought up and I ran into someone I used to know at school. It was very strange because he recognised me and started speaking to me but I had no idea who he was. Then it hit me, he was the bully at my school all those years ago. Now, I draw the line at rudeness but I couldn't believe this person was speaking to me like we were friends after the way he treated me at school. I tried to make my excuses and leave, but he just kept on speaking to me. At least at school you knew where you stood with him because he was so horrible, but now it was strange as he seemed quite friendly; but I couldn't forgive him for the past. I know it was a long time ago and I thought that I'd gotten over it, but it seemed that I still held a grudge against him after all these years.

Phrases:

To bring up (children): this means to raise children. To have and look after children. It is often used as "I was brought up in a (big) family" or "I was brought up in England" etc.
Example: *I was brought up near the sea so I could swim from an early age.*

To run into (someone): To meet someone (usually someone you already know) by chance.
Example: *I haven't seen Bill since school, and then just by chance I ran into him on holiday in France.*

It hit (me): to have a sudden realisation.
Example: *I didn't know why I have been having trouble sleeping recently, then it hit me; the stress of work is causing it.*

To draw the line at…/to draw the line somewhere: this is a way of saying "this is the limit". It basically means that one thing is acceptable but that another isn't.
Example 1: *I don't mind people coming to work a few minutes late, but I draw the line at employees coming in around mid-morning.*
Example 2: *It's difficult to decide what is acceptable and what isn't, but you have to draw the line somewhere, and I've decided that this situation is unacceptable.*

To make excuses: to give (usually fictional) reasons why the situation is bad etc.
Example: *The student was always making excuses as to why he didn't do his homework.*

To keep on: to continue.
Example: *the experiment was a failure but the scientist decided to keep on trying.*

To know where you stand with (someone): This means that the other person is straight forward. Their position is clear. Their meaning is not difficult to understand.
Example: *He may not be very friendly, but at least you know where you stand with him.*

To get over something: This means that you have recovered from a problem or an illness.
Example: *I was sad when I broke up with my girlfriend but I got over it after a few months.*

Part Two

Suddenly, he invited me to go for a drink with him. By this point he was really starting to get under my skin so I said *"no thank you"* but he kept on insisting and eventually I gave in. I know I should have stuck to my guns, but he was being so friendly I started to feel bad about not liking him. Once we were in the bar he started telling me about his life and how he is married to a wonderful woman. I was secretly thinking that maybe her personality had rubbed off on him and that was why he was more pleasant now. When he went to the toilet I thought about making a run for it and leaving him on his own to wonder what the problem was. Then I started daydreaming about payback and all the ways I could take my revenge. When he returned from the toilet I was just about to make an excuse to leave when something very strange happened.

Phrases:

To get under one's skin: This is very negative and describes the feeling that someone/something annoys or angers you and that you can't stop this thing from affecting you.
Example: *I know that he is trying to help, but something about his manner really gets under my skin.*

To give in: this means the same thing as "to give up". So it means when you submit or stop fighting/trying.
Example: A) *Can you guess what I got you for Christmas?* B) *No, I give in, what did you get me?*

To stick to one's guns: This is when you don't back down and you stick to what you believe in. Even if someone tries to change your mind you stay with your opinion.

Example: *I respect people who stick to their guns. I find people who change their minds easily a bit difficult to deal with.*

To rub off on (someone): when you are influenced by someone's attitude or behaviour after spending time with them.
Example: *After spending a week with such a nice family, I hope that some of that good behaviour has rubbed off on Harry.*

Payback: this is used to mean revenge.
Example: *This is payback for lying to me.*

Part Three

Suddenly he started crying! I don't know why but it completely caught me off guard and I suddenly burst out laughing. I didn't want to show him up, but I just couldn't help myself. After a moment I managed to get control of myself and I noticed that he had stopped crying and had stated laughing with me. This of course caused me to start laughing again. After about five minutes we both calmed down and I asked him why he was crying. After a few minutes of beating around the bush he finally got to the point and admitted that he did remember being a bully and had regretted it his whole life. To his credit he did fully apologise, and although we will never be friends I told him that it was water under the bridge. So it was a strange day but I'm glad it happened.

Phrases:

To be caught off guard: when something unexpected happens and you feel unprepared for it.
Example: *She completely caught me off guard when she asked me out on a date. I didn't even think she liked me.*

To burst out laughing: to suddenly start laughing.
Example*: When he fell into the river, I couldn't control myself and just burst out laughing.*

To show (someone) up: to embarrass someone.
Example: *He really showed himself up when he refused to help us with the preparations for the party. I mean it was his idea in the first place.*

Can't help oneself: this describes when you can't control your own actions.
Example: *Whenever I see chocolate, I can't help myself, I have to eat it.*

To beat around the bush: to be very vague and not say exactly what you mean.
Example: *Stop beating around the bush and just say it. What do you really want to say?*

To get to the point: to go directly to the heart of the issue and to talk about it directly. The term can be used as a command/request (not very polite).
Example: *Could you stop beating around the bush and get to the point.*

To (someone's) credit: used to praise someone. This is often used to praise someone you would not usually praise.
Example: *Even though he is a little lazy, to his credit he always studies hard for exams.*

Water under the bridge: when a past problem or disagreement is forgiven or no longer important.
Example: *A) I still really feel guilty about what happened last year. B) You shouldn't, as far as I'm concerned, it's all water under the bridge.*

THE DIVORCE AND THE MARRIAGE

PART ONE

A friend of mine got a divorce <u>a while back</u>. Now, usually this would be a very sad time but in the case of this couple I truly believe that they are <u>better off</u> without each other. They were never really right for each other, I mean they <u>got along</u> at the beginning but there was just something a little off with their relationship. I think my friend <u>hit the nail on the head</u> when he said that basically they were <u>like chalk and cheese</u>. I remember my friend came to me about a year after they got married and told me that things were so bad that they were not even speaking to each other and that he felt that he had to <u>walk on eggshells</u> whenever he was around her. He kept on asking me for my opinion but I kept giving useless advice such as "<u>it's up to you</u>" or "<u>the ball's in your court</u>". The thing was, that I was trying to <u>cover up</u> a secret that I had kept for years.

<u>Phrases:</u>

A while back: this means 'quite a long time ago'.
Example: *I met him a while back, while I was still in college.*

Better off…: this means that your situation is better if…
Example: *Some people think that you are better off not going to university and just getting a job immediately.*

To get along/on: to have a good relationship with someone.
Example 1: *I really get on with my boss.*
Example 2: *I don't get along with my dad.*

To hit the nail on the head: to perfectly sum up/describe an issue/situation.
Example: *When you said that the situation was impossible, I really think that you hit the nail on the head.*

Like chalk and cheese: this means that two people are completely opposite in their personalities.
Example: *Those two are like chalk and cheese but they seem to get along pretty well.*

To walk on eggshells (around someone): when you feel that you have to be overly cautious around someone. Used when someone is overly sensitive.
Example: *He gets so angry over the smallest thing, I really feel like I have to walk on eggshells around him.*

It's up to you: this means that the choice or responsibility belongs to the person that you are speaking to.
Example: *A) I can't decide whether to go or not. What do you think?*
B) I don't know. It's up to you really.

The ball's in your court: this is similar to "it's up to you" but is used more seriously and means that you need to make the next move.
Example: *I've done all I can to fix this problem, now the ball is in your court.*

To cover something up: used when a crime or secret is concealed.
Example: *The bank covered up the insider trading.*
Example:*(Noun): Many people believe that there was a police cover up over that incident.*

Part Two

I had met him in university about 10 years ago when he had <u>shown up</u> uninvited to one of my parties. He had tried to speak to me then but I <u>brushed him off</u>, I was angry that he had <u>gate-crashed</u> my party. The next day he came to my house and apologised. At first I wouldn't accept his apology but in the end he just kept on apologising so I just <u>gave up</u> and <u>let him off</u>. We remained friends until he eventually <u>dropped out of</u> university to start his own company. After that we just sort of <u>drifted apart.</u>

<u>Phrases</u>

To show up/ to turn up: both of these phrases mean 'to appear'. When used with items it usually refers to lost things. When used with people it can refer to someone who was lost or when a person appears in an unexpected place/situation.
Example 1: *I lost my wallet but I'm sure it will turn up somewhere.*
Example 2: *He showed up at my workplace drunk. It was so embarrassing.*

To brush (something/someone) off: to treat something/someone like it/they doesn't/don't matter.
Example: *He just brushed me off like my opinion didn't matter.*

To gatecrash a party: to go to a party that you are not invited to.
Example: *The party was really fun until some gatecrashers turned up and spoilt it.*

To give up: this means to stop doing something/stop making an effort or to lose hope.
Example: *I gave up on him a long time ago; he's just not worth the effort.*

To let (someone) off (for something): this is used when one forgives or doesn't punish someone after they've done something wrong.
Example: *Boss) I'll let you off this time but don't be late again.*

To drop out of (university/college/school): this is when someone quits attending university/college/school. The noun is 'drop out' so 'he's a dropout'.
Example: *My parents are really angry because my brother dropped out of university to become a musician.*

To drift apart: this is used when two people naturally stop seeing each other. They don't really stop being friends they just don't keep in contact any more.
Example: *Me and my brother sort of just drifted apart after he got married.*

Part Three

Anyway, about three years ago I went into a shop to buy a computer and there he was behind the counter. It was great to see him after all these years and he was looking very handsome. I had always regretted that we hadn't dated so I thought I would take my shot now. We spoke for a while and I skirted around the issue but eventually I asked him if he was married now. He told me that he was engaged and then he invited me to his wedding. My heart sank. Anyway, we remained friends but the more I got to know him the more I fell in love. When his marriage was in trouble I tried to not get involved but when he got divorced I confessed my love to him. He told me that he felt the same way. I was on cloud nine, but because he had just got divorced and everything was up in the air I didn't want to get into anything too serious. Anyway, to cut a long story short we took things slow and dated for two years and now we are about to get married.

Phrases:

To take one's shot: This means that you will take your opportunity for something. You have the chance to do something, so you will try your hardest to achieve it.
Example: *When I was at school I had the chance to compete in a national competition. Even though I didn't win, I'm glad I took my shot.*

To skirt around an issue: to not say what you really mean and to talk *around* a subject rather than talking about the real issues.
Example: *It feels like we've been skirting around the issue, but I think that we need to discuss the real issues in detail.*

My heart sank: this describes the feeling of being suddenly very disappointed.
Example: *My son trained very hard for that competition so my heart sank when he lost.*

To be on cloud nine: to be very happy.
Example: *Since I won the award I've been on cloud nine.*

Everything is up in the air: This means that things are undecided. It also has the feeling that things are unsettled.
Example: *Ever since the recession began, everything at work has been up in the air.*

To cut a long story short: this means when you just tell someone the main point or the conclusion of a story without going into all of the details.
Example: *I could tell you all of the details of the trial but that would take forever, so to cut a long story short 'he was found not guilty'.*

THE FASHION SHOW

PART ONE

I know absolutely nothing about fashion, so when my best friend asked me to help her run a fashion show, I knew there was going to be trouble. I think the reason I don't like fashion is that I always thought it was just beautiful people <u>showing off</u>. But anyway she asked me, I agreed, and now I was determined to <u>see it through to the end</u>. Also she asked me before and I had <u>backed out</u> <u>at the last minute</u> so this time I didn't want <u>to let her down</u>.

Phrases:

To show off: to be too proud of yourself and display it in an arrogant manner to get the attention of others.
Example: *He is good at sports but he is always showing off so nobody wants to play on the same team as him.*

To see (something) through to the end: to complete a project even when you don't want to.
Example: *I hate my job but I'm going to see my contract through to the end.*

To back out: this is when you agree to do something and then change your mind and not do it.
Example: *The singer was supposed to play at the concert but backed out because the pay wasn't high enough.*

At the last minute: this means 'at the last possible moment'.

Example: *They were about to get married and then at the last minute the bride got scared and ran away.*

To let someone down: to disappoint someone.
Example: *You really let me down when you didn't come to the party.*

Part Two

Now, my friend is really into clothes, actually you could even say that fashion is her calling in life. She loves to wear really over the top colours but for some reason they always look really good on her. However, in my case, I am a fashion disaster, I have no colour sense whatsoever, I don't even know what size I am. The first task she gave me was to read fashion magazines and find out what was in this season. Obvious I failed at this as I had no idea what the magazines were talking about. After that my friend decided that I was only allowed to help with non-fashion related tasks such as driving the models from the train station etc. Little did she know that I would still cause trouble even if I didn't get close to the actual fashion.

Phrases:

Now,...: this is used when you want to emphasise the beginning of a sentence.
Example: *Now, I wouldn't say he was short but he certainly isn't tall.*

To be 'into' something: this means to be really interested or enthusiastic about something.
Example: *When I was younger I was really into skateboarding.*

(One's) calling in life: to discover one's perfect vocation in life.
Example: *On my first day of teaching, I knew that I'd found my calling in life.*

Over the top: when someone's actions/reactions are much more than is necessary.

Example: *I think firing him was a bit over the top, he only made a minor error.*

In my case: this is used when talking about your own situation/personality/likes and dislikes.
Example: *My wife loves sailing but in my case I'd rather stay on dry land.*

To find out: to investigate and then (hopefully) discover something.
Example: *The teacher rang the parent to find out why the student was absent from class.*

(Duffle coats) are in (this year): this is often used to mean that something is currently popular.
Example: *Perms were really in when I was young.*

Little did s/he /they know: this means that that the person didn't suspect something.
Example: *she was never careful with her money. Little did she know that she was about to lose her job.*

Part Three

On the day of the fashion show, I went to the station <u>as per</u> my friends <u>instructions</u> to pick up the models. I arrived 5 minutes early to be sure that I would be there to greet them when they arrived. After 10 minutes they still hadn't shown up so I started to get nervous. After 15 minutes I decided to ring my friend. She was already quite stressed so I had put off ringing her because I didn't want to worry her any more. When I rang her I told her the models were late, and maybe they had got a later bus. "BUS? What do you mean BUS?" she screamed down the telephone. "You were supposed to meet them at the TRAIN station not the BUS station". I replied "ok ok, <u>keep your hair on,</u> the train station is next to the bus station so I can get there in 1 minute. So I finally got the models to the fashion show but they were so late that they didn't have enough time to put make up on. This actually <u>worked out,</u> as the newspapers thought it was <u>on purpose</u> and reported that it was a very original fashion show. So in the end everything <u>turned out for the best.</u>

<u>Phrases</u>

As per instructions: to follow instructions.
Example: *As per my father's instructions, I will donate half of his money to charity.*

Keep your hair on!!: used when you want to tell someone not to overreact (this is not that polite).
Example: *Ok keep your hair on, it's not that serious.*

(When things) work out: this is used when you think a bad situation will resolve its self. It will get better.
Example: *Whenever I stress about work my wife just says 'don't worry everything will work out fine'.*

On purpose: to wilfully do something. To decide to do something and then do it.
Example: *He said that it was an accident but I think he did it on purpose.*

To turn out for the best: This is similar to 'to work out' and means that even if there were problems, the end result was good.
Example: *I dropped out of university but I started a successful company so it all turned out for the best.*

The End and then the Beginning

Part One

Last weekend it was <u>raining cats and dogs</u> so I decided to be really lazy and just watch loads of TV. Mostly, I just watched soap operas and romantic comedies but there was one documentary that really <u>stuck in my mind</u>. It was all about how one stupid action completely destroyed someone's life and how this person (his name was John) was eventually able to fix his life. The story starts when John was 18 years old. He was apparently very shy but would suddenly lose his temper and get completely <u>out of control</u> if anyone ever tried to argue with him. Anyway, one day he was in a shop, and the shop keeper accused him of stealing. Now most people if they were innocent would just say "I'm sorry but I didn't do anything; you can check if you like". But as per usual his temper <u>got the better of him</u> and he <u>ended up</u> completely destroying the shop. Of course the police were there <u>in no time</u> and arrested him <u>on the spot</u>.

Phrases:

Raining cats and dogs: to be raining really heavily.
Example: *I was supposed to visit my mother but it was raining cats and dogs so I rang and cancelled.*

To stick in one's mind: this means that for some reason you remember a particular thing, event or person.
Example: *The thing that sticks in my mind about school was how much I hated school dinners.*

Out of control: this means that the situation/person has gone wild and can't be controlled.

Example: *She was out of control when she was younger, but she seems very respectable now.*

To get the better of someone: this is used when someone/something has an advantage over someone else. It has the feeling of someone being affected negatively by someone else. So if someone always manages to beat you at something, or if they can always upset you on purpose, we would say that they always get the better of you.
Example: *Even though I try to ignore his comments, he always manages to get the better of me and I end up being stressed.*

Ended up...: eventually this thing happened.
Example: *I started as a waiter but I ended up owning the restaurant.*

In no time: very quickly.
Example: *I started as a regular employee but I worked really hard and was promoted to manager in no time.*

On the spot: immediately, at that location.
Example: *As soon as I met her I knew on the spot that I would end up marrying her.*

Part Two

Although he hadn't hurt anyone, because of the aggressive nature of his crime he was sentenced to one year in Jail. While he was in jail he tried to <u>keep his head down</u> but because he would never back down from any argument he was constantly getting into fights and trouble. Because of this, his prison sentence kept on being extended and he eventually spent 3 years in prison. When he left prison, of course he had to <u>start from scratch</u> as he had no job and nowhere to live. Although he was trying to <u>make a go of</u> his life he felt for a long time that he was <u>taking one step forward and two steps back.</u> He tried to get a job but because of his criminal record it was very difficult, and when he did get a job he would lose it because of his temper. It seemed at that point that he was really <u>going nowhere in life</u>.

<u>Phrases:</u>

To keep one's head down: to keep out of trouble.
Example: *He never gets involved in arguments at work. He just keeps his head down and gets on with his work.*

To start from scratch: this means that you start something from the very beginning. For example if you build a house from scratch, it means that you didn't just fix it, but started building it from the foundations.
Example: *I lost my essay, so I had to start again from scratch.*

To make a go of (something): to make a big effort to succeed.
Example: *Even though my husband and I have been having troubles in our marriage we have decided to make a go of it and try to fix the problems.*

One step forward, two steps back: this phrase is used when you feel that you are not making any progress. So even if you move forward slightly, actually you are moving backwards further. Example: *As much as I try recently, I can't seem to make any progress, it seems like I'm taking one step forward and two steps back.*

Going nowhere in life: to not be making progress with one's life. Example: *After I lost my job I really felt that I was going nowhere in life.*

PART THREE

Then one night it <u>struck him</u> that he had to take control of his life and that his problems were caused by his anger and his temper. He would be doing fine in a job or relationship and then as soon as he <u>came across</u> even a small problem he would completely <u>overstep the line</u> and blow things out of proportion. He realised that he needed to <u>come to terms with the fact that</u> he had a problem, and then do something about it. From that point on he searched for ways to control his anger and finally he found out about meditation. He found that meditation helped him have more self control and be more peaceful. He studied for many years and now he is a famous teacher and travels the world helping other people. I thought that it was a very touching story.

<u>Phrases:</u>

It strikes (me)…: this means that you realise something.
Example: *It strikes me that you would be in a better position if you quit your job and went into business for yourself.*

To come across something: to encounter something.
Example: *I was looking through an old book store when I came across this book on 'fishing'.*

To overstep the line: this is used when someone says or does something that is unacceptable. So if there is a border between what is acceptable and what isn't, this person has crossed over from acceptable to unacceptable.
Example: *I don't mind him criticizing me but he really stepped over the line when he started criticizing my wife.*

To come to terms with something: to accept something as the situation.

Example: *he needs to come to terms with the fact that his wife has left him and she's not coming back.*

THE BIRTHDAY PARTY

PART ONE

I was born on Christmas day, which means that I never really celebrate my birthday. Once in a blue moon I'll go for 'birthday' drinks on Christmas eve with my friends but that doesn't really count. It was worse when I was a kid because all of my friends would have parties for their birthdays but I never got the chance to have one for myself. Also I would always get 'joint Christmas and birthday presents' which basically meant that I would get one present instead of one for my birthday and one for Christmas. I assure you I'm not complaining and I'm happy to receive any presents at all, but when you're a kid you really want to celebrate your birthday. Anyway as the years went by, I stopped paying any attention to my birthdays and I accepted that it was something that I didn't really celebrate. That is, until this year.

Phrases:

Once in a blue moon: very very occasionally.
Example: *I do drink, but only once in a blue moon.*

Doesn't count: this means when an action is invalid.
Example: *That goal doesn't count as he scored after the final whistle was blown.*

To get the chance: be able to. To have the chance to do something.
Example: *I wish I got the chance to meet my grandfather but he died before I was born.*

I assure you: this is another way of saying 'please trust me'. It's used when you want someone to not worry and to believe you.
Example: *I assure you, if it's at all possible there will be no redundancies.*

To pay attention: to concentrate on something.
Example: *Stop talking, and pay attention to your driving.*

Part Two

This year, <u>the same as usual</u>, I was going to my parents house to spend Christmas with them, but then <u>at the last minute</u> my mother rang and cancelled saying that she wasn't feeling very well. I was a little disappointed because I'd already arrived at the train station, but at least I hadn't gotten on the train. Anyway, I returned home and when I got in the front door all of my friends and family were waiting there. They all shouted "surprise!". They told me later that they felt it was <u>about time</u> I got to celebrate my birthday so they thought they would <u>throw me a party</u>.

<u>Phrases:</u>

The same as usual: the same as always.
Example: *I got up at 8 am, the same as usual.*

At the last minute: to do/realise something at the last possible moment.
Example: *I always do my essays at the last minute.*

About time: this means that after a long time of not doing something, it is the right time to do it.
Example: *I haven't cleaned my room in ages so I thought that it was about time I tidied up.*

To throw a party: to have a party.
Example: *We threw a welcome party for our new house guests.*

School Days

Part One

When I think back to my school days, at first I get quite nostalgic and then I come to my senses and remember how much I absolutely hated school. I remember that I liked my teacher and my friends, and I even liked some of my studies, but what I couldn't stand was sitting in the classroom. It used to drive me crazy having to sit indoors in a classroom when I could be outside running around having the time of my life. Although I wasn't badly behaved, I was always fidgeting and daydreaming and never concentrating on the class. My teacher used to always say that I had my head in the clouds.

Phrases:

To think back to/on: this is used when one is talking about one's past.
Example: *I try not to think back on my past and prefer to enjoy the present.*

Come to one's senses: this is used when you suddenly realise that your thinking or actions are wrong or incorrect, and then correct them immediately.
Example: *I almost did a bungee jump and then I came to my senses and backed out.*

Can't stand: this means to hate something/someone.
Example: *I can't stand travelling, I always get sick.*

To drive one crazy: this means to make someone very angry or frustrated.
Example: *I hate this actor, his arrogance drives me crazy.*

Have the time of one's life: to have a great time.
Example: *I had the time of my life on holiday.*

To have one's head in the clouds: to always be daydreaming and never concentrating on real life.
Example: *If he didn't always have his head in the clouds he would probably make a success of his life.*

Part Two

The only thing that I did like at school was sports class because I got to let off steam and run around for a while. Also, the only teacher that <u>saw potential</u> in me was Mr Jones, the sports teacher. He always said that when I ran he'd 'never seen anything like it before'. He also started giving me extra training and got me to race in a few local competitions. By the time I was 11 I was winning all of my races so my parents decided to send me to a special sports academy. While I was there I was completely <u>in my element</u>. We did train a lot at that school but it wasn't like we were outside from <u>sun up to sun down,</u> we did have to spend some time in the classroom. All of the teachers there understood that we all wanted to be professional athletes and <u>went out of their way</u> to help us achieve that goal. I made a lot of friends at that school but when it came to competitions 'friendship' <u>went out the window</u>. <u>At the end of the day,</u> we all just wanted to win.

Phrases:
To see potential in someone/something: to see that someone/something could be successful in the future even if it is not that way now.
Example: *When everybody else thought that the project was a failure, I saw that there was some real potential in it.*

In one's element: to be really comfortable with a situation/action etc.
Example: *A lot of people are scared of racing cars, but I'm in my element on the race track.*

Sun up to sun down: all day.
Example: *I train sun up to sun down.*

To go out of one's way (to help someone): to really help someone more than you have to.
Example: *The students went out of their way to help the new student get used to the school.*

(For something to) go out the window: this refers to a time when usual rules or agreements are discarded when the situation changes.
Example: *During the divorce any type of goodwill towards each other went out the window.*

At the end of the day: this means 'in the end'. The eventual situation was/is….
Example: *Even though we are divorced, at the end of the day we will always be friends.*

Boy Hears Girl

Part One

I have never been what you would call a ladies man. It's not that I don't like women or that I don't want to go out with them, it's just that I've never been that confident. Because of this, my mother is always worrying about me and trying to fix me up with people from her work. Anyway, a few years ago I was just on my way home from a disastrous date with someone my mother had set me up with when I decided to stop at a bar to drown my sorrows. I was sitting at the bar when I heard a woman talking on the phone. I didn't mean to eavesdrop on her conversation, but there was something about her voice that caught my attention.

Phrases:
Not what you would call: this phrase is used when you want to politely say that the person or thing is completely different to the 'adjective' or 'noun' that follows the phrase. So for example, *'She's not what you would call hardworking'* means that she is not at all a hard worker. She is lazy.
Example 1: *He's not what you would call handsome.*
Example 2: *She's not what you would call 'a good employee'.*

Ladies man: this phrase describes a man who is very popular with women. They are good at flirting and very confident around women.
Example: *My cousin is such a ladies man. He's always got a new girlfriend every time I see him.*

To go out with someone: this means 'to date' someone. To have a romantic involvement with someone. It's more commonly used in

British English while 'to date' is more common in American English.
Example: *I went out with a famous celebrity while I was at university.*

To fix someone up (with someone else): this is when someone introduces two people to each other who may (in the future) like each other romantically.
Example: *My sister fixed me up with her husband's best friend.*

To set someone up (with someone else): in this context it means the same as 'to fix someone up'.
Example: *I tried to set him up with my best friend but it didn't work out.*

To drown one's sorrows: this means to drink alcohol in order to forget about your troubles.
Example: *After my divorce I spent about two months just drowning my sorrows.*

To eavesdrop on someone's conversation: this is when you secretly listen to someone's conversation without their permission or knowledge.
Example: *She was a very jealous wife, she used to eavesdrop on her husband's telephone calls to make sure that he wasn't having an affair.*

To catch one's attention: this means that you noticed something. That you became aware of something.
Example: *While all of the actors were good in that film, it was the actress that played the girlfriend that really caught my attention.*

Part Two

I tried to <u>mind my own business</u> but my attention kept drifting to the woman's voice. She was basically <u>pouring her heart out</u> to her friend about how she had just been <u>dumped by</u> her boyfriend. It turned out that her boyfriend had cheated on her and when she confronted him he just <u>broke up with</u> her. It was strange listening to her because although she was upset, there was a real dignity to her voice and I was sure that she would be fine eventually. After about 30 minutes of <u>listening in on her conversation</u>, I had completely forgotten about my terrible date and all of my other problems. Anyway, I decided that it was time to leave and left without ever seeing her face.

Phrases:
To mind one's own business: this is used to describe when one does not interfere with someone else's affairs/life. It means to not be nosey.
Example: *I try not to get involved in office politics, I just mind my own business and do my own work.*
Note: It can be used as a phrase when you want someone to stop interfering in your life or to stop them from asking personal questions. For example:
Person one) Why were you fired?
Person two) Mind your own business!

To pour one's heart out: this is when you tell someone all of the emotional details about a story or about your feelings.
Example: *He is a very cold father, even though his son poured his heart and explained what was wrong, the father just ignored him.*

To dump someone/ To be dumped by someone: this is used when one person ends a romantic relationship with another. It is quite a

negative way to say that the relationship has ended and it was because one person wanted it to end.
Example: *He is usually the one who dumps the other person but this time it was his girlfriend who dumped him.*

To break up with (someone): this is a more polite way to say that a romantic relationship has ended. Also you can use this phrase if it was one person who wanted to end it or both people.
Example 1: *My boyfriend broke up with me last week.*
Example 2: *Me and my boyfriend broke up last week.*

To listen in on someone's conversation: this means the same as to eavesdrop on someone's conversation.
Example: *You shouldn't listen in on people's private conversations. It's very rude.*

Part Three

Anyway, about two years ago my mother tried to set me up with another girl from her work. Of course I refused but she <u>wouldn't take no for an answer</u> and eventually I gave in and agreed to go on the date. I met the girl at a local café and we chatted a little. She was very pretty but I knew that it wouldn't come to anything so I didn't try to flirt or anything and I knew that as per usual I would just end up in <u>the friend zone</u>. After about half an hour I had a real feeling that I'd met this girl before but I couldn't <u>place her face</u>. Then I suddenly realised that it wasn't her face I recognised but her voice; it was the girl from the bar a few years earlier. I told her this but she didn't believe me. So I recalled all of the details that I'd overheard. She was completely <u>floored</u> that I remembered her voice. Anyway, this really <u>broke the ice</u> and we had a wonderful date. We eventually <u>wound up</u> dating and eventually got married. My mother is very pleased!

Phrases:
To not take *no* for an answer: to insist on something.
Example: *He always insists on paying for dinner, even if you argue with him, he won't take no for an answer.*

The friend zone: this phrase is often used by young men. It describes the situation where you want to have a romantic relationship with a girl but you slowly end up just being friends with her.
Example: *I feel sorry for him, he's such a nice guy and he always ends up in the friend zone, whereas other total idiots always get the girl.*

To place someone's face: this is often used as 'I couldn't place (his) face' and it means that you recognise their face but you don't know where from.

Example: *There was a picture of the criminal on the television. I recognised him but I couldn't place his face. Then I remembered that he went to the same school as me.*

To be floored: to be completely surprised/shocked.
Example: *I was completely floored when I realised that I hadn't got the promotion.*

To break the ice: this phrase means 'to start a conversation' with someone who you haven't met before . It has the feeling of a very polite/formal conversation that becomes friendly/fun for some reason. Although it sounds negative, it actually isn't.
Example: *When I first meet someone I try to break the ice by saying something funny and making them laugh.*

To wind up (somewhere): this means 'to end up' somewhere or doing something. It is usually used when the outcome was unexpected.
Example 1: *I wound up living in the desert.*
Example 2: *Even though we didn't like each other at first, we wound up best friends.*
Example 3: *Most people said that I would probably eventually get fired but I wound up being the boss.*

THE DEAD END JOB?

PART ONE

Recently I was made redundant from a company I'd been at for about ten years. <u>The thing is</u>, my job had pretty much dominated my life, so losing my job was a big shock. At first I was a complete mess and didn't know what to do with myself. I spent all day just lazing around <u>feeling sorry for myself</u>. After about <u>a month or so,</u> I decided that enough was enough and I started to <u>pull myself together</u>. I started by reconnecting with some old friends that I'd drifted apart from while I'd been so busy at work. It was nice at first seeing all of those old friends but I quickly noticed that actually we no longer had anything in common so I stopped seeing them and went back to not doing much. After a while my redundancy money started to run out and I needed to get a job. I <u>searched high and low</u> but couldn't find anything suitable. I applied to a few good jobs but eventually I just gave up. I'd <u>hit rock bottom</u>, I had no job, no money and no real friends.

<u>Phrases:</u>
The thing is: this is used to emphasise a point. When you want the listener to pay attention to the point you are making.
Example: *I would quit my job, but the thing is…I'm in debt and really need the money.*

A (month/week/day/hour/minute) or so: this is used to mean 'around/about (a month etc)'.
Example: *They knew each other for a week or so before they got married.*

To feel sorry for oneself: to pity yourself.

Example: *It has been over a month since he lost his job, he should stop feeling sorry for himself and get out and get another job.*

To pull oneself together: this means to 'get your life together'. To stop wasting time or worrying and fix your life.
Example: *He hasn't washed since he was dumped last week. He needs to pull himself together and get his life back on track.*

To search high and low for something: to look everywhere for something.
Example 1: *I searched high and low for a good job in my town but eventually I had to move to London.*
Example 2: *I searched high and low for a specific engine part to fix my car. I eventually found it in an online shop in France.*

To hit rock bottom: to be at the worst point of your life.
Example: *Sometimes you need to hit rock bottom before you realise that you need to change the path you are on.*

PART TWO

Eventually I decided the best thing for me to do was to join a temping agency. Initially working for the temping agency was absolutely awful, but I told myself that it was temporary and that I just needed something to keep the wolf from the door. Basically, as a temp you just go from company to company filling in for employees who are absent. Most of the jobs were very boring; a bit like watching paint dry. However, sometimes you just get jobs which no one else is willing to do. After about two months of temping I was asked to go and work the night shift at a local storage warehouse. At this point I was pretty much living hand to mouth so I couldn't really refuse.

Phrases:
To keep the wolf from the door: This phrase means that you are doing something just to make enough money to survive. It usually describes a temporary situation. It usually describes a job/activity that you are only doing because you have to.
Example: *After I lost my construction job, I worked in a cement factory just to keep the wolf from the door until I got another construction job.*

To fill in for (someone): this is when you do something instead of the person that usually does it.
Example: *Susan was sick today so George filled in for her.*

(It's) like watching paint dry: Very *Very* boring.
Example: *I don't know why people love his films so much, I find they're like watching paint dry.*

Pretty much: this means the same thing as 'basically'.

Example: *They live with each other, they own a house together and they have kids, so they are pretty much married even if they haven't done it officially.*

To live hand to mouth: this describes the situation where you are only just earning enough money to survive.
Example: *While I was starting my company I was living hand to mouth for about 4 years until it became successful.*

Part Three

The night shift at the warehouse was from 10pm until 6am. On my first day I turned up with a sense of dread as I was seriously not looking forward to working there. The only thing that kept me going was the thought that it was only temporary. When I arrived I went to the main office to introduce myself but there was nobody around. I waited there for about half an hour but no one showed up so I set off to try to find someone. The warehouse was absolutely huge and filled with old house stuff that people had stored there while they were living abroad. I walked around for a while but still couldn't find anyone. Eventually I heard someone shout "I've found you!....I win!". Then suddenly about five people popped up from nowhere. I asked them what on earth were they doing? They told me that they had been playing 'hide and seek!' I was totally surprised as they were all ages, ranging from 20 to about 60.

Phrases:
A sense of dread: the feeling that something bad is going to happen. A feeling that you are entering a bad situation.
Example: *Every time I'm called into a meeting I get a sense of dread.*

The thing that kept me going: the thing that kept me motivated.
Example: *Even though I wanted to quit, the thing that kept me going was knowing how disappointed I'd be if I just quit.*

To show up: this means 'to appear' or 'to arrive'.
Example 1) *I couldn't find my keys buy they eventually showed up under my desk.*
Example 2) *He was fired because he kept on showing up late for work.*

To set off: to leave to go on a (long or short) journey.

Example 1: *I usually set off for work at around 7am.*
Example 2: *When I was 21 I set off on my around the world trip.*

To pop up: to suddenly appear.
Example1: *I've noticed that lots of new coffee shops have popped up in my local area.*
Example 2: *She scared me because she popped up out of nowhere while I was having lunch in the park.*

What on earth are/is s/he/ they doing?: this is used when you can't believe or completely don't understand what the person is doing.
Example: *He is totally in debt but keeps buying his girlfriend presents. I don't know what on earth he is thinking.*

Note: Hide and seek is a children's game where everyone has to hide and then one person has to go and find everyone.

PART FOUR

It turned out that there was next to nothing to do on the night shift. There just needed to be someone there in case something happened, but nothing ever did. Because the staff were so bored they had had the idea that to kill time they should play games all night. It was absolutely brilliant. Some of the games were old favourites like 'hide and seek' and '20 questions' but they had also invented lots of games such as 'furniture slalom' where you had to race through all of the old junk and make it to the other end as quickly as possible. The other thing about this job was that because it was the night shift it was actually quite well paid. Eventually I got a full time job there and have been there ever since. So out of the blue I have gone from having no job and no friends to having both. And now of course I'm really good at playing hide and seek!

Phrases:
To turn out: eventually 'this thing' happened/was discovered. It is usually an unexpected outcome.
Example 1: *I didn't want to go to that party but it turned out to be quite fun.*
Example 2: *It turns out that he was stealing from his company.*

There's next to nothing to do: this means that there is very little to do.
Example: *I went to help him get his shop ready for the opening but there was next to nothing to do.*

To kill time: to fill empty time. To keep occupied when you have nothing to do.
Example: *We had a stop-over in Korea on our flight to Japan so we killed time by looking at the duty free shops.*

Ever since: from (a certain time), this condition has remained the same.
Example: *Ever since I was at school I have wanted to be a chef.*

Out of the blue: completely unexpected.
Example: *Completely out of the blue I received a cheque for £100*

FAKE

Part One

My friend was recently telling me about her boss and how she is so horrible that she now wants to quit her job. Now, my friend has always prided herself on being an excellent judge of character, so I think that she is probably right about her boss. However, as to whether she should quit because of it, I feel that she has let her emotions cloud her judgement. Essentially, both my friend and her boss used to be friends and they started at the company at the same time and at the same level as each other. They both made their way up the ranks and after a few years they were both 'Heads of Department'. They were both successful and got on really well. Then suddenly the Head of the Company decided to step down. Both my friend and her 'then' friend wanted the job but were worried that it would come between their friendship so they both decided that they would back down and neither of them would apply for the job.

Phrases:
To pride oneself on (something): this is used when one feels that an aspect of their personality is good. Or they feel they have a certain skill.
Example: *Italians usually pride themselves on their cooking.*

A good judge of character: this phrase means exactly what it says; that one is good at judging other people's personalities and characters.
Example: *He was never a good judge of character and was always doing business deals with really untrustworthy people.*

To cloud one's judgement: this is when you are not thinking clearly and you do something (stupid or wrong) that you wouldn't usually.
Example: *I think that the stress of work has started to cloud his judgement and he keeps on making stupid mistakes.*

To make one's way up the ranks: this means that you steadily get promoted higher and higher in a company/organisation (or of course the military).
Example: *He started as an apprentice then made his way up the ranks until he was the CEO.*

To step down: to willingly stop being the boss. This can sometimes mean that the person has left the company/organisation but not always.
Example: *The Prime Minister stepped down due to family reasons. The Deputy Prime Minister will take over until the elections.*

Then (husband/job etc): this phrase is quite common and means the same thing as Ex-, but is used when talking about a specific time in the past. For example: *When I lived in America 2 years ago, my then job was to teach Maths….but I have a different job now.*
Example: *When I worked for ABC company my then boss was Charles Downs.*

To back down: this is when you are in a confrontation and you or the other party concedes.
Example: *He's so stubborn that even if he's obviously wrong he won't back down.*

To come between (two people's) friendship: this is when an event (or someone) becomes a problem and causes people to no longer be friends.

Example: *Even though they were friends since childhood they still let a woman come between their friendship.*

Part Two

My friend had totally forgotten about the whole 'promotion' thing when suddenly there was an announcement that the other woman had gotten the job. My friend couldn't believe her ears! Surely this was some kind of mistake? She dropped everything she was doing and went out to find her soon to be EX-friend. When she confronted the other woman about stabbing her in the back the woman just hid behind crocodile tears and said that she needed the money and that she didn't think my friend would care that much.

Phrases:
Can't believe (my/her etc) ears: this is used when you can't believe what you are hearing. This is not used concerning a lie but usually in response to something shocking.
Example: *I couldn't believe my ears when I heard that the Prime Minister was resigning.*

To drop everything: to suddenly stop what you are doing and then (usually) go and do something else.
Example: *When I heard that he was in the hospital, I dropped everything and went straight there.*

To stab someone in the back: to betray someone.
Example: *He stabbed his friend in the back for money, but now of course no one trusts him.*

Crocodile tears: fake tears.
Example: *Stop with the crocodile tears, I know that you are just trying to manipulate me.*

PART THREE

From that point on things pretty much went from bad to worse. My friend tried to come to terms with the betrayal but try as she might she just couldn't forgive the other woman. Work had become unbearable for her so she was now on the verge of tears every time she got up in the morning. I tried to explain that it wasn't the end of the world and that everything would work out for the best, but my friend was basically at the end of her tether and was desperate to quit her job even though she loved it and had worked so hard to get to where she is. Anyway, to cut a long story short, eventually the other woman was fired because she was 'untrustworthy', and my friend was promoted to the top job. It just goes to show 'honesty is the best policy'.

Phrases:
From that point on: this means 'from then on' but is used to emphasise the point.
Example: *I found out that my employee had been taking fake sick days. From that point on I never really trusted him.*

To go from bad to worse: this simply means that things started pretty bad and then just got worse and worse.
Example: *After my divorce things just went from bad to worse and I ended up losing my job.*

To come to terms with (something): to accept the situation as it is.
Example: *It took me a long time to come to terms with losing my job.*

Try as (s/he etc) might (s/he etc) just couldn't…..: this means that even though they really tried, they were not able to succeed in something.

Example: *Try as I might I never could get used to driving, so now I just take the bus.*

On the verge of tears: almost at the stage when you will start crying.
Example: *I think that he is way too sensitive, he always seems to be on the verge of tears whenever you disagree with his opinion.*

It isn't the end of the world: this phrase is used when you want to say that the situation is not that bad.
Example: *Even though he's lost his job, it's not the end of the world; he'll get another job.*

Everything will/it will work out for the best: even though it doesn't seem like it now, eventually everything will be fine.
Example: *Even though I lost my job, everything worked out for the best because I got a much better job in the end.*

To be at the end of one's tether: to have no more patience or energy left for a certain situation. To be emotionally exhausted.
Example: *The baby had not stopped crying for 2 days. The mother was completely at the end of her tether.*

To cut a long story short: this is used when you just want to 'sum up' a story quickly. To cut out the details and describe basically what happened.
Example: *It was a really long game, but to cut a long story short; we lost!*

It just goes to show: this means 'this is proof that (something is the case)'.
Example: *The fact that he was unsuccessful for so many years but is now very rich, goes to show that if you are persistent enough success will come in the end.*

Honesty is the best policy: it's best to be honest.
Example: *People who lie always have stress in their lives so I always think that honesty is the best policy.*

A Tale of Three Careers

Part One

I was in the shop the other day when a magazine article <u>caught my eye</u>. The story <u>centred around</u> a middle aged man who had had a very eventful life. He was born into a very poor family where they <u>could barely make ends meet</u>. When he was very young he would go out doing odd-jobs for people in the local neighbourhood or sell lemonade to his classmates. Basically, he would do <u>everything in his power</u> to help his family <u>get by</u>. Due to his strong will, he eventually got a full scholarship to a top university where he studied business. After university he didn't get a great job but he was working for a large famous firm so at least it was <u>a foot in the door</u>. After his bosses realised what a hard worker he was, they quickly promoted him. His rise was so quick that he was soon regarded as a <u>rising star</u>. Everybody thought that he would be running the company in a few years. But even though he had lots of money and a successful career something was wrong.

Phrases:
To catch one's eye: this phrase is almost always used as '(it) caught my eye'. It basically means the same as 'caught my attention' but is used with visual things. If you are window shopping and you see a coat that gets your interest you would say that it 'caught your eye'. Example: *He was such a good footballer as a child that he quickly caught the eye of a few of the major clubs and he was soon signed to one of their junior sides.*

Centred around (something): this means that the article or film is about (something). It can also mean that this (something) is the main thing in the story or incident.

Example 1: *The film centres around a young boy with special powers.*
Example 2: *The court case centred around whether the defendant had a good alibi or not.*

To make ends meet: this means to make enough money to survive and pay the bills etc. It usually has the feeling of 'only just' surviving.
Example: *Even though I have two jobs I can only just manage to make ends meet.*

To do everything in one's power: to do everything you can possibly do in order to achieve a certain outcome.
Example: *The police did everything in their power to catch and convict the killer.*

To get by: this is very similar to 'make ends meet'. It is however slightly more positive and can mean slightly above 'just surviving'.
Example: *I don't have a lot of money, but I do get by without too much trouble.*

To get a foot in the door: this means to get a first opportunity to do something (work in a specific field/company etc). It is usually used when you start low (at a company etc), but there is opportunity to move higher.
Example: *Even though it's a boring job I just see it as a foot in the door to an industry that I want to work in.*

A rising star: this is someone who is fast becoming popular or famous in a certain field or company.
Example: *Even though he is young and quite inexperienced he has become a rising star since he closed that big deal for the company.*

Part Two

The problem was that although he had pulled himself out of poverty he always had a funny feeling that something was missing from his life. Eventually he decided that he probably just needed to work for himself. When he was younger he always had an entrepreneurial spirit so he thought that if he just started his own company he would feel complete again. Although he could have gone in a completely different direction, he decided that it was a case of 'better the devil you know' and started a finance company. Due to his hard work and excellent business acumen his business went from strength to strength. After working all the hours that god sends he decided enough was enough and sold the company for a huge amount of money. Although he enjoyed retirement, that old feeling of having something missing quickly started to return.

Phrases:
To have a funny feeling (that…): to feel something through intuition.
Example: *I had a funny feeling that she was untrustworthy, and as it turns out; I was right.*

Better the devil you know: this means that it is better to stick with someone/thing that you know (even if it/they are not perfect), rather than trying someone/thing completely new (and unknown).
Example: *I could move to a new country but I always think that it's better the devil you know, so I'll probably just stay here.*

Business acumen: this is not really a phrase (it's more of a collocation), but it is very useful. It means that someone has a real talent for business.
Example: *When he started his business he didn't have much money but he did have very good business acumen and a few good connections. This meant that he was destined to be successful.*

To go from strength to strength: to get better and better.
Example: *The Batman films just go from strength to strength.*

All the hours that god sends: to do something every available hour.
Example: *When I was younger I worked every hour god sent to get my business started, but now I'm able to take it a little bit easy.*

Enough is enough: this is used when one is no longer willing to accept something which is undesirable.
Example: *I put up with my brother's bad moods when we were kids but when we became adults I just thought 'enough is enough' and now I just try to avoid seeing him if possible.*

PART THREE

One day a few months after he had sold his company he suddenly had a burning desire to return to the area that he had grown up in. He was walking along when he noticed that there were lots of buildings which used to be shops but were now just lying empty. He knew that this was a very poor area and that there was a huge problem with unemployment, so he decided then and there to do something about it. He gathered local community groups together and started a business advice service. There he would give advice and help with funding for young people who wanted to start their own businesses. Now that area is completely thriving and people from far and wide come there to go shopping. He has completely improved both the area and the lives of people who live there. Also at the end of the article he said that even though he liked making money and working in finance he always felt that he was just going through the motions. Now that he is working for the community and changing people's lives he's found the one thing that was missing all those years; passion for what he was doing.

Phrases:
(To have a) burning desire: this is a desire that you cannot stop. It usually pushes you into taking action.
Example: *I always had a burning desire to go to India, so when I was 30 I spent 6 months working there.*

Far and wide: a large area. This is used when speaking about a product/service or fame.
Example 1: *People came from far and wide to see the concert.*
Example 2: *He is known far and wide as a great motivational speaker.*

To go through the motions: this is when you just do the bare minimum with no enthusiasm.

Example: *Even though it was good money I just felt like I was going through the motions so I quit my job and trained to become a therapist.*

The Art of Negotiation

Part One

I've often wondered about what makes a good negotiator. Is it just a case of being good at talking or having a strong will, or is it something more than that? In my line of work I often have to negotiate on price with suppliers. Usually I offer a much lower price and then they (most times) start to come down on price. Then we usually end up meeting somewhere in the middle. Of course there are some people who won't negotiate and try to hold their ground, but they are usually trying to make a point rather than just trying to get a higher price. They think that if they negotiate it's a 'sign of weakness' and people will try to take advantage of them. These people are pretty rare and most will, when push comes to shove, come down on price.

Phrases:
Line of work: this means 'field of work'. It does not usually mean 'job title' but more 'type of job'. For example if someone asks "what line of work are you in?" you would answer "banking" and not "I work for ABC Bank".
Example: *After the recession I decided to try a new line of work.*

To come down on price: to lower the price. This is usually used when referring to a negotiation.
Example: *Even though it was overpriced he just refused to come down on the price and eventually he lost the sale because he was too stubborn.*

To end up: eventually this thing (will) happen (happened).
Example 1: *People who lie always end up getting caught.*

Example 2: *I started rich but because I wasn't careful I ended up living in poverty.*

To hold one's ground: to not back down on your point. To not give in. To remain strong when arguing your point.
Example: *Don't let your boss bully you around. Just hold your ground and he will eventually get tired and just leave you alone.*

When push comes to shove: this phrase describes the point where you have to do what your heart says. When you have to do what you have to do.
Example: *When push comes to shove I will always be loyal to him, even if I don't always agree with his policies.*

Part Two

Actually, I was on holiday in Morocco once and I noticed that the people there love to barter. Just after I'd arrived there I went shopping in a local market and wanted to buy a decorated plate. I asked the shopkeeper how much it was and he told me it was about the equivalent of $3. To me this was very reasonable so I immediately agreed. It was weird because he seemed a little uncomfortable. When I got back to the hotel I told the story to the manager there. He told me that people there expect you to <u>knock them down on price</u> and actually enjoy bartering. After that, I literally <u>have never looked back</u> and always try to get the best price possible.

Phrases:
To knock someone down on price: this is used when you convince someone to give you a lower price on something.
Example: *If you ever buy a second hand car, make sure that you knock them down on the price as no one expects you to pay full price.*

To have never looked back: this means that some event changed your attitude and from that point on you have done things differently.
Example: *I have never looked back since I discovered online gaming. Now not only is it my hobby, but I have also built a successful business around it.*

Does Ambition Equal Happiness?

Part One

Is it wrong to be un-ambitious? I once worked with a group of young people who had absolutely no ambition whatsoever. It used to <u>drive me nuts</u> because it felt like they just <u>took life for granted</u> and never put any effort into anything. I often said to them "<u>the world is your oyster,</u> why don't you go out into the world and do something with your life?" They would always say "oh no I could never do anything, I don't have any money". Eventually I just gave up trying and in the end I <u>lost touch with them</u>.

Phrases:
To drive one nuts: this is used when something makes you very annoyed or angry.
Example: *Some dance music is good but most of it just drives me nuts.*

To take things for granted: this is when you think that it's a normal state of affairs and attach no value to something. It is a negative phrase and used when someone doesn't value something that is actually valuable.
Example: *He always took his wife for granted until she had enough of his demanding attitude and left him. Now he sees what he has lost.*

The world is your oyster: this phrase means that you can have what you want and achieve anything if you just try.
Example: *Why are you wasting your time doing this low paid job. Now that you have your qualifications the world is your oyster.*

To lose touch with (someone): to lose contact with someone. Example: *I lost touch with all of my school friends, but now through social networking websites I've gotten back in touch with some of them.*

Part Two

After that, I moved up to London and started to mix in different circles. At the time I was just trying to get my business off the ground and was mixing with other entrepreneurs. The difference between the young people I'd met before and these young entrepreneurs was like night and day. Everybody was very focused on their own business and were determined to do whatever it took to make their business a success. I used to love speaking to them because their motivation and enthusiasm really had an effect on me. After a while, a few of my entrepreneur friends became successful, so in their case all that hard work paid off. But unfortunately others weren't so lucky and their businesses bit the dust.

Phrases:
To get (a business/project) off the ground: to get something started so that it is up and running. It may not be successful yet but it is a running business.
Example: *It's hard work getting a new project off the ground, but it's so rewarding once it's up and running.*

Like night and day: this is used when two things are completely different from each other.
Example: *Julie and her husband are like night and day when it comes to their political views, but they seem to agree on everything else so their relationship seems to work well.*

When (something) pays off: this is when the result of hard work is very good. When you benefit from your hard work.
Example: *Even though it is a risk to start your own business, if the risk pays off you will be much more financially secure.*

To bite the dust: to die. This can mean 'to actually die' or can be used when a project, company or relationship dies.

Example: *Most of these fads just bite the dust after a few months but that diet plan is still going strong after 2 years.*

Part Three

Now that I'm a little older I can see both sides of the story. Some people could be considered to be un-ambitious but actually they are just happy with their lot. I for one think that there is nothing wrong with ambition as long as you keep a level head and are not too disappointed when you meet with setbacks. I'm sure that those young people I met years ago are happy and that's what counts. But in my case I feel that it is better to have a goal as it keeps life interesting.

Phrases:
To be happy with one's lot: to be content with your life.
Example: *Even though I'm not rich I am definitely happy with my lot.*

I for one: 'others may not agree but in my opinion....'
Example: *After the way he has been acting lately, I for one will not be buying his new album.*

To keep a level head: to not get too excited or angry. To stay calm and see things clearly.
Example: *When dealing with aggressive people it's best to keep a level head and not get into an argument with them.*

To meet with setbacks: this means that an obstacle has slowed or stopped your progress. Some people just say 'to meet setbacks' which is less grammatically correct but still commonly used.
Example: *It's normal to meet with setbacks when starting a new business, but you must try to keep going.*

THE TIME TRAVEL RECORD SHOP

PART ONE

Where have all the old record shops gone? You've probably noticed that over the past few years all of the record shops have started disappearing. At first it was because all of the big chain stores were taking over. But now since everyone downloads music online the loss of sales has even taken its toll on the larger high street shops. No one even really buys CDs anymore let alone vinyl. Anyway, recently I came across a record player in a second hand shop and then on a whim I bought it. When I got home I realised that it was a complete impulse buy because I didn't even have any records to play on it. Of course the record player just sat in the corner of the room, unused and gathering dust. Whenever my children asked me why I didn't just throw it out I just said that it made me feel nostalgic and that I liked having it even if I never used it.

Phrases:
To take over: this means to take control of something. It also can mean to dominate a certain field.
Example 1: *I don't like her husband, whenever he's around he always take over and dominates the conversation.*
Example 2: *Japanese car manufacturers have completely taken over in the car market.*

For something to take its toll: this means that by doing something there has (in the end) been a bad effect or outcome. So for example if you drink a lot of alcohol, at first it will be ok but after a while it will 'take its toll' on your liver.
Example: *Years of being a workaholic and never seeing his family have finally taken its toll and his wife decided to divorce him.*

Let alone: this phrase is very difficult to use. It means that A is 'negative' so B would be 'really negative'.
Example 1: I don't like cooked fish let alone raw fish, so there's no way I'd eat sushi.
Example 2: I'm scared to go on buses let alone planes.

On a whim: to do something without really thinking about it beforehand. To do something just because you 'feel like it'.
Example: *I wanted to go to university but I choose to do Geography on a whim.*

Impulse buy: this is more of a collocation than a phrase. It means when you buy something without thinking about it. It is often something that you don't actually need or want.
Example: *To encourage impulse buys many items are priced at .99c so people don't think deeply before buying it.*

Part Two

This summer I went to Brighton for a few days. Brighton is a fashionable town on the south coast of England. It has a shopping area called 'The lanes' which has loads of independent shops. Some of them are <u>run of the mill</u> while others are completely <u>off the wall</u> like the 'bonsai shop' or the 'environmentally friendly toy shop'. While I was <u>milling about</u> <u>I stumbled upon</u> a great record shop. Going in there was like stepping back in time, there were lots of old band posters from when I was young. It was a real 'blast from the past'. I started flipping through the old LPs (long player vinyl records) and began to feel like a teenager again. Each record I came across reminded me of a certain time in my life. I found an old Bob Dylan record which reminded me of the time I cycled around France when I was a teenager. I used to listen to that record constantly while I was travelling around. I also found an old Nirvana record which reminded me of my college days; going out all night to parties and then going straight to class in the morning without sleeping.

<u>Phrases:</u>
Run of the mill: this means 'normal/ordinary' for the thing it is connected to. For example a 'run of the mill day' is a normal day. Example: *Most pop songs nowadays are pretty run of the mill but occasionally you get one which is very inventive.*

Off the wall: completely inventive and different. Very imaginative and not like other things at all.
Example: *Many people feel that Cirque Du Soleil is very off the wall.*

To mill about: to wander around aimlessly. This is used in both a positive and negative light.

Example: *I hate going to shopping malls as there are too many people just milling about doing nothing.*

To stumble upon (something): to find something unexpectedly. This is usually used with places rather than things.
Example: When *I was in Rome I stumbled upon one of the best cafes I've ever been to.*

PART THREE

While I was in the shop I completely <u>lost track of time</u> and spent hours reminiscing about my past. I have never been what you would call 'sentimental', but I really enjoyed my <u>trip down memory lane</u>. After a while I had chosen about 50 records that I wanted to buy. I eventually <u>came to my senses</u> (once I realised that it would <u>break the bank</u>) and <u>narrowed it down to</u> my 10 favourites. When I got home I thought that I would be playing the records <u>around the clock</u> but actually I just sort of forgot about them and they just sat there unused with the record player. I think the thing that really affected me was not the actual music itself, but the act of just standing in the record shop browsing for hours, which is how I spent a lot of my teenage years.

Phrases:
To lose track of time: this is when you are concentrating so much on what you are doing that you forget what time it is.
Example: *I love speaking to him so much, he's so interesting that I always lose track of time when I'm with him.*

To come to one's senses: this means when you are consistently doing something and then realise that it's the wrong thing to do.
Example: *After years of trying to fix our relationship, I finally came to my senses and broke up with her.*

(To take) a trip down memory lane: this refers to when you think about or talk about the past. It is usually caused by looking at something or visiting somewhere. The phrase describes a really nostalgic feeling.
Example: *Going back to my old school after all these years was a real trip down memory lane.*

To break the bank: to spend too much money.
Example 1: *Because all of the items we sold are faulty, reimbursing all of the customers will really break the bank.*
Example 2: *Throwing a party will be expensive but it will hardly break the bank.*

To narrow something down: to start with many possibilities and then after elimination chose one (or a few) option(s).
Example: *There are about ten courses that I would like to do but I need to narrow down my options to those that I can use to get a job with later.*

Around the clock: all the time. This doesn't always literally mean 24 hours a day but it can do.
Example 1: *When my brother was seriously sick, my parents were at the hospital around the clock.*
Example 2: *Some children need around the clock supervision.*

TEENAGE RUNAWAYS

PART ONE

This week the newspapers have been dominated by the story of two runaway brothers. Basically <u>what started as</u> teenage stupidity <u>ended as</u> a national manhunt. These brothers had tried to impress two of the local girls by taking them for a drive in their father's car. Unfortunately they forgot to ask their father for permission to borrow the car and he reported it stolen to the police. Once the brothers realised what had happened they decided to hide until the issue had <u>blown over</u> because they knew their father would <u>hit the roof</u> once he realized what had happened. So they <u>dropped the girls off</u> at their houses and then drove to a local forest behind their house where they thought they would <u>lie low</u> for a few hours.

Phrases:
What started as (one thing) ended as (something else): this describes when a situation changes from one circumstance to another. It sometimes describes a situation that is getting worse.
Example: *What started as a light shower soon turned into a rainstorm.*

To hit the roof: to be crazily angry. This has the feeling of someone suddenly becoming uncontrollably angry.
Example: *My mum hit the roof when she saw the phone bill.*

To blow over: this is when a bad situation passes and it is no longer considered bad any more.
Example: *My mum and dad had a huge argument, I was hoping that it would just blow over, but after 2 weeks they are still not talking to each other.*

To drop someone/thing off: this is when you give someone a lift in your car (or on your bike) and you 'deliver' them somewhere. It is also used with items as well.
Example 1: *When I was hitch-hiking in France people usually dropped me of as close to the town as possible.*
Example 2: *I borrowed my friend's lawnmower so I have to drop it off at his house this morning.*

To lie low: this either means to stay out of the way and not to get into trouble or to hide away.
Example 1: *The criminal lied low until everyone had forgotten about his crime.*
Example 2: *Julie's still angry with me so I might just lie low until she forgives me.*

Part Two

By about 10pm that evening the father noticed that both of his sons were missing. I found that strange that he immediately noticed the car was missing but it took him about 7 hours to notice his sons were not there either! It was at this point that things really started to get out of hand. He rang all the boys' friends but they said that they hadn't seen them. He also called the two girls but they didn't want to drop the boys in it so they covered for them by playing dumb. At this point the father started to jump to all the wrong conclusions and imagine all sorts of awful things so eventually he rang the police. Because both the car and the boys were missing the police put two and two together and concluded that the boys had run away.

Phrases:

(For something to) get out of hand: this means that the situation has gotten out of control. It describes a situation that maybe wasn't great but is now very bad.
Example: *I went on a peaceful march but then a few people started throwing things and things very quickly got out of hand.*

To drop someone in it: this is a slang term meaning when you tell person 1 that person 2 has done something bad. This then causes person 2 to be in trouble.
Example: *My brother really dropped me in it and told my mother that I wasn't at school today.*

To cover for someone: in this case this phrase means to lie in order to protect someone. However (in another use) it can also mean when you do someone's work when they are absent.
Example 1: *My brother was always getting in trouble at school so I had to cover for him when my mother asked about him.*
Example 2: *My workmate was ill so I had to cover for him by doing overtime.*

To play dumb: this means to pretend that you don't understand or that you have no idea what the other person is talking about.
Example: *Even though he was obviously guilty, the suspect just played dumb and hoped that the police would not find enough evidence.*

To jump to the wrong conclusion: this is when you see all of the evidence but misunderstand it and come to the wrong conclusion.
Example: *Henry saw his girlfriend with another man and immediately assumed she was cheating on him. But he had jumped to the wrong conclusion because the other man was actually just her brother.*

To put two and two together: this is when you reach the right conclusion after looking at the situation/evidence.
Example: *When I went to work this morning, people were acting strangely around me and the boss asked to see me privately. I put two and two together and assumed that I was about to be fired.*

Part Three

By the next morning the boys still hadn't shown up, so a national manhunt started. By this point the girls realised that things had gotten completely out of hand and decided <u>to come clean</u>. The police then checked the local forest and found the boys <u>fast asleep</u> in the car. It turned out that the boys were planning to go home after their dad had gone to bed but they fell asleep waiting. When they were found they were <u>oblivious to the fact</u> that they had caused so much trouble. When they got home, although the father was glad they were safe, he <u>went totally bananas</u> and <u>read them the riot act</u>. Both of them have been grounded (are not allowed out) until they are 18 and they are never allowed to ever use their father's car again. It just goes to show, things can get out of hand pretty quickly if you are not careful.

<u>Phrases:</u>
To come clean: to admit to something.
Example: *My little sister said that she didn't break my doll but she felt so guilty that she eventually came clean and confessed.*

To be fast asleep: to be completely asleep.
Example: *I was fast asleep when the doorbell rang.*

Oblivious to the fact (that): to be completely unaware of something.
Example: *He was oblivious to the fact that his wife was cheating on him for over 2 years.*

To go bananas: this means to get very angry. To go crazy.
Example: *He's going to go bananas when he realises that he didn't get the promotion he was promised.*

To read someone the riot act: to get very angry with someone. This can also mean to get angry and then tell someone off and lay down rules.

Example: *When my husband realised that I was so in debt he read me the riot act and banned me from using credit cards.*

Never a Lender or Borrower Be

Part One

I'm pretty easy going but if there's one thing I draw the line at it's lying. I've got a pretty close knit group of friends and I'd like to think that I know them all very well. But what do you do when two of your friends fall out? Do you try to help them patch things up or do you take sides? Like most groups of friends there are some people that you get on with better than others. In my case the ones that I'm closest with are Mark and Johanna. The only problem is, is that they don't always see eye to eye. Mark is pretty serious while Johanna is more outgoing and fun. Anyway, everything was going along fine with our friendship group until Johanna suddenly stopped showing up whenever Mark was around.

Phrases:
To be easy going: to be relaxed and easy to get on with.
Example: *He's a pretty easy going guy, not at all stressful to be around.*

If there's one thing (that I hate/annoys me....it's...): this is used to emphasise something that you dislike.
Example: *If there's one thing that scares me, it's horror movies featuring ghosts.*

To fall out with someone: to stop being friends with someone.
Example: *I fell out with my sister when I was about 18 years old.*

To patch things up: to mend/fix something. This is often used to mean to mend a relationship; to become friends again.

Example: *Me and my husband are going to try and patch things up. Neither of us wants a divorce.*

To take sides: when two people/parties are arguing or fighting you choose one side and defend/join that side.
Example: *As a teacher it's best not to take sides when children are arguing with each other.*

To see eye to eye: to agree with someone's opinion/point of view. Often used as 'we <u>don't</u> see eye to eye'.
Example: *Even though we don't always see eye to eye, we both want what is best for the company in the long run.*

Close knit group/family: this means that the group/ family has a very close relationship.
Example: *That company is a very close knit group. Not only do they work together they also socialise and go on holiday together.*

Part Two

At first I didn't even really notice but then slowly <u>it dawned on me that</u> <u>something was up</u>. I asked Mark what was going on, but he just said "it's nothing, don't worry about it". Anyway I sort of forgot about it until one day I was out with Johanna and I managed to get her to <u>spill the beans</u>. Apparently Johanna had lent Mark some money about a year ago. She was expecting him to pay her back pretty quickly but the whole thing started to <u>drag on</u> so she decided to ask him what the <u>hold up</u> was. He just kept saying that he'd pay her back soon, but then he never did.

<u>Phrases:</u>
To dawn on one that: to suddenly realize that something is the case.

Example: *After going on holiday to Italy it dawned on me that I never even ate a pizza the whole time I was there.*

Something is up: this means that something is wrong/different/strange about a situation.
Example: *I knew something was up because he's usually quite unfriendly but this time he was quite nice. It turns out that he needs my approval to get the promotion.*

For something to drag on: this is when something lasts for *too* long.
Example: *I know everyone loves Lord of the Rings but I found that it drags on a bit.*

To spill the beans: to tell a secret. To give details on a private subject. This phrase is more common in British English.
Example: *Are you and John dating? Go on spill the beans!*

A hold up: a delay. When something delays something else.
Example: *I've been stuck in traffic for 2 hours, I have no idea what is holding everything up.*

PART THREE

At first Johanna wasn't too worried as she had plenty of money and she thought Mark was <u>good for it</u>. But slowly she started to wonder when *and if* she was ever going to get repaid. Also, she felt completely <u>in the dark</u> because Mark never tried to contact her or assure her that he was definitely going to pay her back. Then <u>out of the blue</u> Johanna lost her job and she had to live off her savings and then her credit cards. After a few months all of her credit cards were completely <u>maxed out</u> and she could no longer <u>make ends meet</u>. She tried to tell Mark about how serious her situation was but he kept on <u>fobbing her off</u>. In the end I decided to <u>stop sitting on the fence</u> and try to fix the situation. I rang him and told him to pay her the money or our friendship would be over. Even though he did return the money eventually, the whole thing <u>left a bad taste in my mouth</u> so I tend to try to avoid him nowadays.

Phrases:
To be good for it: this means that you will definitely pay back a loan.
Example: *I usually don't lend money to people but I know he's good for it so I lent it to him.*

To be in the dark about something: to not know what is going on in a certain situation.
Example: *I have no idea what we are doing on my birthday, my wife has kept me completely in the dark about her plans. She says that it is going to be a surprise.*

Out of the blue: unexpectedly.
Example: *I hadn't seen him for about 10 years and then he showed up out of the blue at my birthday party.*

To sit on the fence: this is when you do not take a position on either side of the argument. You do not take sides.
Example: *I hate that political party because they are always just sitting on the fence. They never take risks and stand for something they believe in.*

To fob someone off: to not give someone a direct answer. To give an excuse so as to avoid the real issue. This phrase is difficult to use.
Example: *Every time the journalist asked the politician about the economy he was just fobbed off with meaningless clichés.*

To make ends meet: to make enough money to live on/to pay the bills etc.
Example: *Minimum wage is just about enough to make ends meet.*

To max out credit cards: This is when you have completely used up all of your overdraft or are at the limit on your credit cards.
Example: *Recently, people are maxing out their credit cards in order to pay their mortgage.*

To leave a bad taste in one's mouth: when something happens and it leaves you with a bad attitude towards that thing.
Example: *I used to like his films but after he made that really sexist film, it just really left a bad taste in my mouth and I didn't want to see any of his later movies.*

REALITY TV! REALITY?

PART ONE

I'm not going to <u>mince my words</u>; I absolutely hate Reality TV. I don't know if you have it in your country but here in England, watching it is almost a <u>national pastime</u>. If you don't know what reality TV is, it's basically a type of <u>fly on the wall</u> documentary (and I use 'documentary' <u>in the loosest sense of the word</u>) where you watch people going about their daily lives. However, now there are lots of different types of these shows and some of them <u>are anything but</u> based on reality.

Phrases:

To not mince one's words: to say things directly. This is used when you tell the truth and do not try to be polite to make people feel better.

Example: Even though my boss seems a bit rude and never minces his words, at least you know where you stand with him.

A national pastime: this is used to describe an activity that a certain nationality is well known for. It is often used for something slightly unusual.

Example 1: *Moaning about the weather is a national pastime in Britain.*

Example 2: *Being overly polite is almost a national pastime in Canada.*

To be a fly on the wall: the main way to use this phrase is '*I'd love to be a fly on the wall when ……is/was happening*'. This means that you would like to secretly observe a certain situation. For example, '*I hate George, I'd love to have been a fly on the wall when he got fired*'. This means that you would have liked to watch this thing happen.

Note: In the story above we used '*fly on the wall documentary*' this is a documentary that observes the everyday life of people.

Example 1: *I hear that she is going to confront her husband about the affair tonight. I'd love to be a fly on the wall when that happens.*

Example 2: *Recently there are more and more fly on the wall documentaries on TV. I think it's because they are cheap to make.*

In the loosest sense of the word: this means that 'technically' something is true but in reality things are a bit different.

Example 1: *In my opinion car racing is only a sport in the loosest sense of the word, I mean even golf is more active than that.*

Example 2: *You could call me an American but only in the loosest sense of the word. I mean I was born there and have an American passport, but I've lived my whole life in England so I consider myself to be British.*

To be anything but: this means that the thing is definitely not as described. So **A** is the total opposite of **B**.

Example 1: *In the advertisement it says that the film is suitable for children, but it is anything but. I mean there was lots of violence and bad language.*

Example 2: *I thought the film was anything but boring, even though all the reviews said it was. I thought that it was really interesting.*

Part Two

There are hundreds of different shows but as far as I can tell there are roughly only three types.

Type one: This one is a type of competition. Basically they get a group of people together and they have to do activities to win a prize. The most famous is called 'Big Brother'. This is where a group of people have to live together in a house for a certain amount of time. They are complexly <u>cut off from</u> the outside world and have no entertainment other than to talk to each other. Usually what happens is certain small groups emerge and then all they do is sit around gossiping about each other. Also after a while everyone gets <u>cabin fever</u> and starts <u>to act up</u>. It's really boring to watch but people love the voyeuristic aspect of the show and get completely <u>hooked on</u> it.

Type two: This type is similar to the one above but it follows 'normal people' around in their everyday life. There is no competition aspect but it still seems fake. These people often become sort of celebrities (even though they have no real talent!) and tend <u>to milk</u> their <u>15 minutes</u> as much as they can by doing advertisements and endorsement deals with various brands. The most popular of these shows are 'Made in Chelsea' which is a 'semi-reality' show about rich <u>20-somethings</u> and 'The Only Way is Essex' which is basically the same thing but about poorer 20-somethings.

Type three: This one I can just about stand. This is where they place cameras in schools or hospitals and the like, and show what life is like in this type of environment. These programmes have a bit more value as they kind of show the <u>'behind the scenes'</u> of different situations. They are less voyeuristic and seem closer to a real documentary than the other two mentioned. The most famous is 'One Born Every Minute' which is about babies being born in hospitals.

<u>Phrases:</u>

To be cut off from (something): to not have access to something. This often means that you have been denied access to something. Also: to be 'cut off' can mean that you no longer receive money etc from your family.

Example 1: *The people of Bhutan are cut off from western technology.*

Example 2: *His parents have completely cut him off.* He no longer gets any financial help from them.

To have cabin fever: to be stuck in a small area for a long period and to go a bit crazy. This often refers to an enclosed space, but not always.

Example: *I liked living on that small island but I got cabin fever after a while.*

To act up: to behave a bit badly. This phrase usually refers to children's behavior.

Example: *He's usually ok but he starts to act up if he gets too bored.*

To be hooked on (something): to be addicted to something. This can mean actual addiction like 'hooked on drugs', or just as a way to describe an emotion like 'hooked on selling things on Ebay'.

Example: A lot of people in that town are hooked on drugs because there is no work and nothing to do, so they start taking drugs out of desperation.

To milk something: to exploit a situation. This is when you try to get the most value as possible out of a situation. It is a bit of a negative term and means that the person is trying to get a bit too much. It is often used as the phrase: 'to milk something for all it's worth'.

Example: *My son was sick for a few days but now he's really milking it and trying to stay off school even though he's basically feeling better.*

15 minutes (of fame): this phrase was coined by Andy Warhol and means 'temporary fame' or fame for no real reason. It has the feeling that the person has no real talent. Note: people often just say '*15 minutes*' and leave off the '*of fame*'.

Example 1: *I hope she enjoys her 15 minutes of fame because it won't last.*

Example 2: *I think that pop star's 15 minutes are almost over, nobody is that interested in her any more.*

20/30 etc-something: this means that you are between 20-29, 30-39 etc.

Example: *I hate going to that bar because it's always full of 20-somethings, it makes me feel so old.*

Behind the scenes: how things actually work. What happens in the places you would not usually have access to. So for example a behind the scenes look at how a movie is made will show exactly what the makers do to produce a film.

Example 1: *People always complain about the bus service but behind the scenes it takes a lot of work to keep the busses running on time.*

Example 2: *That documentary is a behind the scenes look at the food industry.*

Part Three

Now even though I hate these shows, my family absolutely loves them and sometimes if I have nothing else to do I watch them. last week I was watching Made in Chelsea and it <u>occurred to me</u> that while this show is a complete waste of time for me, it would be brilliant for those who want to learn English. Mostly they just talk about relationships and gossip about each other, but the phrases they use and the way they speak is, on the whole, pretty natural. The problem with learning English from dramas etc is that they are all scripted so are not 100% natural, but with these 'reality' shows they just say whatever <u>pops into their heads</u>. Also if you find a show that is fun, you are more likely to want to watch it and it won't feel so much like studying. <u>So there you have it</u>; I have finally found a use for terrible 'Reality' TV...it turns out that is perfect for learning English with.

Phrases:

To occur to one: to suddenly have a thought. To suddenly think of something.

Example: *As I will be visiting Italy anyway it occurred to me to I could visit the house my mother was born in. I think that would be interesting.*

To pop into ones head: when a thought suddenly appears in your head. In the above article it is used as 'to say whatever pops into your head' this means to <u>not think</u> before you say something.

Example 1: *I have no idea how I knew the answer, it just sort of popped into my head.*

Example 2: *He should be more careful how he speaks to people. He just says whatever pops into his head and usually ends up offending someone.*

So there you have it: this is usually only used in writing or in stories. It is used in conclusion to sum something up.

Example: *So there you have it, the story of how the leopard got it's spots.*

SPREAD BETTING

PART ONE

Someone was recently telling me about Spread Betting. I'm not surprised if you've never come across this, but it is pretty interesting and my friend's experience of it was certainly <u>a cautionary tale</u>. Before I tell you about what happed to him I'll just <u>let you know</u> what Spread Betting is. Essentially it is a kind of financial betting where you place bets on whether a certain market or share will go up or down in price. Now this sounds like <u>a piece of cake</u>, but <u>needless to say</u> it's not simple at all. Basically for every point the share or market goes up or down you will gain or lose the amount you have bet. So if you bet £1 a point and the share goes up 100 points you will gain £100 but if it goes down 100 points you will lose £100. So it's easy to make big money but just as easy to <u>get into hot water</u> and lose lots of money.*

*Disclaimer: The above description of spread betting is not 100% accurate, and was written to illustrate how to use 'English phrases' and not spread betting . Please consult a financial professional before making any investment decisions.

<u>Phrases:</u>

 A cautionary tale: a story that you use as an example of when something goes wrong. Used to illustrate what *not* to do.

Example: *That film is a cautionary tale of what happens when someone is too greedy.*

To let one know: to inform someone of something.

Example: *I'll let you know before Friday what time the party starts.*

A piece of cake: very easy.

Example: *Once you get used to it, riding a bike is a piece of cake.*

Needless to say: of course this is the case.

Example: *The politician made loads of promises before the election, but needless to say he never delivered on any of them.*

To get into hot water: to get into trouble. This has the feeling of being quite serious trouble.

Example: *He doesn't like to talk about his youth but I think he got into some pretty hot water with the police at one time.*

Part Two

Anyway, my friend John has always been interested in economics and a few years ago he decided to buy a few company shares on the stock market. He basically did no research and just picked them at random, and through pure blind luck he made a small fortune. Of course this would be great if he had just left it there but by this point he was convinced that he was a stock market genius. So he decided that he would try Spread Betting. Now the thing about spread betting is that it is 'leveraged' which means that you can easily go into debt. So only people who know what they are doing should attempt it; and John had no idea what he was doing. Most sensible people would open a practice account so they could get the hang of things, but not John, he just dove in to the deep end using real money on a real account. As you can imagine, his confidence mixed with his lack of knowledge plus the fact that it is easy to get in debt was a recipe for disaster.

Phrases:

Blind luck: complete luck.

Example: *It was blind luck that I found his house at all. The street wasn't even listed on a map.*

A small fortune: a large amount of money.

Example: *I made a small fortune when I sold my house.*

To get the hang of things: to get the knack/trick of doing something. To get used to/good at something.

Example 1: *It took me a while to get the hang of living in such a hot country but I really like it now.*

Example 2: *Once you get the hang of it, driving a car is pretty easy.*

To jump in at the deep end/to be thrown in at the deep end: this means to go fully into a situation or action. Not to slowly enter but to fully commit to something. It sometimes has the feeling of rushing into something. Note: To 'jump in the deep end' means that it is your choice. To be 'thrown in' means that someone has made you do this thing.

Example 1: *She always jumps in at the deep end with relationships and usually ends up living with the guy after only a few weeks of going out with them. That's why it rarely lasts.*

Example 2: *When training new employees I like to throw them in at the deep end; that way they learn much quicker and become more self reliant.*

Example 3: *The new recruits were thrown in at the deep end and had to go and make sales on the first day.*

A recipe for disaster: this is when all of the aspects (or ingredients) of a situation mean that things will definitely go wrong.

Example: *That country has an unstable government and the people are very angry, it's definitely a recipe for disaster.*

Part Three

In spite of the fact that all of the manuals say that you should make a plan and then stick to it, John just rushed headlong into trade after trade with no idea of what he was doing. He was ok for a while but soon he started to make huge loses. After a while he had not only lost all of the money he made on just buying normal shares, but had also gone quite seriously into debt. John usually has nerves of steel but at this point he was seriously stressed. He eventually bought a book and followed what it said religiously and by the skin of his teeth was able to get back his loses and is no longer in debt. Hopefully now that he has broken even he will give up and get a less stressful hobby, but knowing John I doubt it.

Phrases:

In spite of the fact: this means the same as 'even though'. So the situation may suggest one outcome but in reality another outcome will occur/has occurred. It has the feeling of going against what most people would expect.

Example: *In spite of the fact that he is only 5 foot tall, he has become one of the most famous basketball stars in the world.*

To stick to something: to keep doing something even if it is difficult. This is often used as 'stick to the plan'.

Example 1: *At first I found leaning English difficult but I just stuck to it and now I'm fluent.*

Example 2: *If we just stick to the plan, I'm sure everything will work out fine.*

To rush headlong into something: this means to rush into something without thinking first.

Example: *When starting a new business people tend to rush headlong into it without researching the market first. That's why lots of business go bust so quickly.*

To have nerves of steel: to be brave. To not scare easily.

Example: *You need nerves of steel to do a bungee jump.*

To follow something religiously: this is when you follow something exactly/closely. It can be used for following instructions or following the news etc.

Example 1: *The thing about cookbooks is that if you follow the instructions religiously the food will taste perfect but all of the ingredients will cost a small fortune.*

Example 2: *I have been following the events in the Middle East religiously.*

By the skin of one's teeth: only just. Barely.

Example 1: *I didn't study very much at university and only graduated by the skin of my teeth.*

Example 2: *He was very close to being fired and only managed to keep his job by the skin of his teeth.*

To break even: to make back the money you have invested in something. To have no profit or loss after a certain enterprise.

Example: *When you start a new company it usually takes at least a year to break even.*

The Secret? The Lie?

Part One

I don't get upset easily but <u>I'm pretty fed up</u> with people who lie. <u>Some might say</u> that <u>there's a fine line between</u> keeping a secret and lying but until recently I felt that it was pretty <u>clear cut</u>. Anyway, in my area there is a young unemployed guy called Tim of about 25 who lives near me. He always seems to be <u>hanging around</u> and not doing much. One day he asked me if I needed any work doing. Usually I'd decline but I felt like giving him a chance so I got him to clean my garden. I was on my way out so I gave him the key to the shed and told him to get on with it. I was <u>cutting it a bit fine</u> for work so I didn't get the chance to go into detail about what needed doing before I had to run off.

Phrases:

To be fed up with something: this is when you no longer have patience for something. You've had enough of something.

Example: *I'm totally fed up with his rudeness, next time he says something to me I'm going to scream.*

Some might say: this means that 'this is an opinion some people hold'. It doesn't necessarily mean that you hold this view as well.

Example: *He's very old, some might say that it's time that he retires and lets someone else run the company.*

There's a fine line between A and B: this means that even though **A** and **B** are different the line between them is not always clear. It's often used to illustrate that a situation or event could be viewed in a negative way.

Example: *There's a fine line between being pushy because you want someone to achieve something and actually bullying them.*

To hang around: this means to wait/stand around not doing much.

Example 1: *The man asked the police to hang around until he was sure that the threat had passed.*

Example 2: *I hate going shopping with my wife as I just end up hanging around waiting for her.*

Clear cut: very clear.

Example: *He was the clear cut winner.*

To cut it fine: to almost be late for something. For example if it usually takes at least 10 minutes to get somewhere and you only have exactly ten minutes to get there then you are cutting it fine. You may be *on time* but only just.

Example: *It's Christmas eve and I still haven't bought any presents. As per usual I'm cutting it a bit fine.*

Part Two

While I was at work it completely slipped my mind that he'd been working on my garden. So it was a pleasant surprise when I saw what a good job he had done. After that I got him to do my garden on an as and when basis. Also, that summer at my work, the caretaker retired so I suggested to Tim that he apply for the Job. At first he wasn't up for it but I convinced him that it was better than just wasting his time all day sitting around. Eventually he applied for the job and got it, but he always seemed to be a bit uncomfortable. At first I thought that it was just a case of taking time to settle in, but after a few months of working there he was still acting strangely.

Phrases:

To slip one's mind: to forget something. This has the feeling of being temporary and about something that is not that important .

Example: *I'm sorry that I forgot to return the library book, it completely slipped my mind.*

On an as and when basis: this means that this thing will happen at different times and dates when it is needed. It is not on a schedule. For example if you clean your car every week then that is not 'as and when'. However if you clean it whenever it gets dirty then you can say 'I clean it on an as and when basis'.

Example: *I go food shopping on an as and when basis, there's no real schedule.*

To be up for something: to be keen to do something.

Example: *Are you up for going to France this weekend?*

Note: Be very careful when using this as it can sometimes refer to sexual activities.

To settle in (somewhere): to become comfortable somewhere. To get used to living (etc) somewhere.

Example: *It took me a while to settle in when I moved schools but I like it here now.*

Part Three

One morning I arrived at work and discovered that Tim had been suspended from his job. I went to my boss and asked him what had happened. He told me that Tim had lied on his job application so my boss needed to investigate further. I was really angry with Tim, I mean I had stuck my neck out and vouched for him so that he could get the job in the first place. I did a bit more investigating and it turned out that he had a few skeletons in his closet. When he was 18 he had got into trouble with the police for stealing and had done time for it. That evening I got a message from Tim saying that he wanted to clear the air. When I met him he explained that he was so ashamed about going to prison that he never wanted anyone to know about it. So that was why he didn't want to apply for the job, he basically didn't want to let on about his past. While I was still angry, I didn't want one mistake that he'd made years before destroy his life so I convinced my boss to take him back. Even though I still hate lying, I now understand that things are not always so clear cut.

Phrases:

To stick one's neck out: to take a risk. It is usually related to taking a risk on a venture or a person. It is **not** used with risky physical activities such as rock climbing.

Example: *I could have stayed in my comfortable job, but I decided to stick my neck out and try something new.*

To vouch for someone: to give a personal guarantee that someone is ok/suitable for something. Usually used when you want to say that someone is trustworthy. Often used in relation to employment.

Example: *If I didn't think he was capable of doing the job, I wouldn't have vouched for him.*

In the first place: initially. At the beginning.

Example: *Why are you blaming me for the bad restaurant, I didn't want to go there in the first place.*

To have skeletons in one's closet: to have secrets in one's past. Usually related to dark secrets.

Example: *That guy is always judging others but I bet he's also got a few skeletons in his closet.*

To 'do' time: this means to spend time in prison/jail.

Example: *I heard that he did time when he was living in Australia.*

To clear the air: to try and fix a disagreement you have with someone. To clear up a misunderstanding.

Example: *Me and my brother fell out last year but my mother brought us together so that we could finally clear the air.*

To let on: to disclose something. To reveal something.

Example: *Even though he was pretty upset when his wife left him, he never let on. He just pretended that everything was fine.*

The Personality Makeover

Part One

I have a cousin Bill who for <u>all intents and purposes</u> is not a very nice person. I'm not sure how it came about but at one point he went from being annoying to being unpleasant to be around. My other cousin Sue, thinks that it's <u>down to</u> a bad relationship that left him pretty bitter. One of the most difficult things about him is that he <u>takes almost everything personally</u> and can be offended by even the slightest thing. I kept on telling him that '<u>you reap what you sow</u>' and that if he <u>kept it up</u>, he'd end up alone with no friends or family. Anyway, it got to the point where I just felt like I was <u>beating a dead horse</u> so I gave up and avoided seeing him.

Phrases:

For all intents and purposes : this means that *this* is basically the case. It may not be 'officially' the case but it is 'in reality' the case.

Example: *He has been suspended from his job without pay, so for all intents and purposes <u>he's been fired</u>.*

Down to: because of….

Example: *The reason they won was down to teamwork.*

To take something personally: to be offended by something. To have your feelings hurt by something.

Example: *Don't take this personally but I think that you need to find a new line of work.*

To reap what you sow: this means that if you do something wrong then bad things will come as a result of those bad actions. If you do bad things (sow) you will get bad things (reap).

Example: *I wasn't surprised when the dictator was imprisoned for life, I mean you reap what you sow.*

To keep something up: to continue doing something.

Example: *Learning a language is difficult at first but if you keep it up, you will become fluent.*

To beat a dead horse: to keep saying the same thing to the point where you are tired of saying it. This usually means that you are trying to make someone understand but they just don't seem to 'get' what you are saying.

Example: *I keep telling him that he needs to take his job seriously or he will get fired but I feel like I'm beating a dead horse because he just ignores me.*

Part Two

About a year ago I heard through the grapevine that Bill had pretty much burnt all of his bridges and that nobody would have anything to do with him anymore. I know that it's bad but I kind of thought that it served him right. To be fair, he couldn't care less about anybody else so why should they care about him? You could say that it was a taste of his own medicine. Although I didn't wish him ill, I certainly had no desire to ever see him again.

Phrases:

To hear something through the grapevine: to indirectly hear some news but not from the person etc it is about. This is a bit like a rumor but has more of a feeling of truth to it.

Example: *I heard on the grapevine that my ex-husband has just remarried.*

To burn one's bridges: to destroy a relationship. To no longer be able to have dealings with someone because that relationship ended badly.

Example: *When you leave a job, it's best not to burn your bridges as you will definitely need a reference in the future.*

(I/s/he etc) couldn't care less: to not care at all about something. This is used in quite a negative way.

Example: *I couldn't less who started the argument I just want you two to stop shouting at each other because you are giving me a headache.*

A taste of one's own medicine: when one experiences similar problems/distress as they cause other people.

Example: *My boss is so horrible but his new boss is even worse, so it's like a taste of his own medicine.*

To wish someone ill: to wish bad things on someone. This is used as 'I don't wish them ill' or 'I wouldn't wish them ill'.

Example: *Even though we are not friends, I'd never wish him ill.*

Part Three

Anyhow, last week I was just doing a little shopping when I heard someone shout out my name. I froze when I realized that it was my cousin Bill. After a bit of an awkward silence we started chatting and to my amazement he was pretty friendly. I have never been very subtle so I just <u>blurted out</u> "What happened to you? Why are you being so nice?" He thought this was pretty funny and wasn't offended at all which would have been his usual response a year ago. He explained that when he realized that he'd lost all of his friends, and his family were avoiding him, it was a real <u>wake-up call</u> for him. He realized that it was <u>high time</u> that he sorted himself out and stopped blaming everybody else for his problems. He decided to <u>tackle his problems head-on,</u> so he bought hundreds of self-help books and also employed a life coach. Anyway, he explained that even though he still had some work to do he was feeling much better. I have to say that I actually enjoyed speaking to him and may even invite him over for Christmas dinner!

<u>Phrases:</u>

To blurt something out: to say something (without thinking first) that you shouldn't say.

Example: *Whenever she's drunk she just blurts out things that are supposed to be secret.*

A wake-up call: here it means when something happens to cause you to realize that you are messing things up. You realize that you need to change your behavior.

Example: *He was out drinking and partying all the time, so when he started getting liver trouble it was a real wake-up call. He has now stopped drinking.*

High time (that something happened): this means that this *thing* should happen. Actually you could say that the *thing* is a bit late.

Example 1: *They have been together for 15 years so it's high time that they live with each other.*

Example 2: *You are 25 years old, it's high time that you move out of your mother's house.*

To tackle one's (problems) head-on: to deal with your (problems) directly.

Example: *If you ignore the problem it will just drag on. It's best to just tackle these things head-on.*

UNREQUITED LOVE

PART ONE

I think one of the hardest things about growing up is when you first have your heart broken. I was speaking to a friend of mine who has a 21 year old son. He absolutely adored this girl that he met at University but she was a bit hot and cold with him. One minute she was all lovey lovey and the next it was as if he didn't even exist. Every time he was just about to give up on her, she would say that she had feelings for him and string him along for a while. But after a while go back to giving him the cold shoulder.

Phrases:

To (run) hot and cold: this means that the person is friendly one moment and the next they are suddenly very unfriendly. You don't know if they will be nice one time you see them and horrible the next.

Example: *I dislike his girlfriend, she always runs hot and cold, you never know where you stand with her.*

To have feelings for someone: this specifically means to have 'romantic' feelings towards someone.

Example: *He always denied it but I'm sure he had feelings for my cousin.*

To string someone along: this means to keep someone interested in something even though you will never give that thing to them. To deceive someone (over a long period of time) into thinking they will receive something. This is used in connection to both romantic relationships and other circumstances.

Example: *His boss strung him along with a promise of promotion even though he had no intention of ever giving it to him.*

To give someone the cold shoulder: to be cold to someone. To ignore someone.

Example: *I eventually had to break up with her because she just gave me the cold shoulder whenever she didn't get her own way.*

Part Two

Apparently this <u>state of affairs</u> lasted for about six months until he heard that she'd actually <u>hooked up</u> with one of her tutors. At this point he decided to <u>cut his losses</u> and <u>call it a day.</u> Although he was heartbroken he was able to direct his emotions into writing a collection of songs about unrequited love. He released an album which ended up <u>going viral</u> on YouTube and he is now enjoying the beginnings of fame. Of course the girl <u>caught wind of</u> the fact that he was becoming successful and tried to get back with him. But this time he'd gotten over her and thankfully he's got enough sense to <u>steer clear of</u> her.

<u>Phrases:</u>

A state of affairs: this means the same thing as 'situation' but it usually refers to a bit of a bad situation.

Example: *My parents never really spoke to each other. That state of affairs lasted until I left home and then they just got a divorce.*

To hook up with someone: this means to kiss or have sexual relations with someone. This word is only used by younger people. <u>Note:</u> This phrase is difficult to use so I would avoid trying to use it in conversation, but it is good to know for listening purposes.

Example: *The stars of that reality TV show are always talking about hooking up with each other.*

To cut one's losses: to decide that you have lost enough and to stop what you are doing.

Example: *My business was extremely in debt so I decided to cut my losses and declare bankruptcy.*

To call it a day: to stop doing something. To call a stop to something. This can be used for long term relationships and projects or for shorter term things.

Example 1: *I've been at work since 7am so I think that I'm going to call it a day and go home.*

Example 2: *After years of trying to negotiate with that country the diplomat decided to call it a day and close the embassy.*

(For a video/song etc) to go viral: this phrase means that a video etc has suddenly become very popular on the internet. Lots of people are sharing it with their friends or on blogs etc.

Example: *The video of the man being rescued in a storm went viral and had 500,000 hits within a day.*

To catch wind of something: this means that you hear about something. It has the feeling of hearing about something indirectly.

Example: *I caught wind of the riots while I was on holiday in that country so I left immediately.*

To steer clear of something: to stay well away from something.

Example: *I used to love chocolate but now that I'm older it's easier to put on weight so I steer clear of it now.*

Do Children Still Play Outside?

Part One

I lived for many years abroad so when I finally returned to England I got what you might call reverse-culture shock. It was the small things that got me at first, like the fact that it is ok to wear shoes indoors or that men instinctively hold doors open for women. But after I got used to all of that there were still a few things at the back of my mind that I couldn't quite put my finger on. One of the things I noticed was that there were no children playing out on the streets any more. Also I noticed that my friends were always ferrying their kids around to one event or another. This was in stark contrast to when I was younger. My mother would always tell us to "to stop getting under my feet" and to "make yourselves scarce".

Phrases:

What got me/What gets me: this means that something affected you. That you noticed something slightly odd. This is often used for things that you don't particularly like .

Example 1: *I wasn't particularly offended by what she said, what got me was the way she said it in that arrogant manner.*

Example 2: *What gets me about politicians is that they do one thing and say the complete opposite.*

At the back of one's mind: this means that deep down you are thinking this thing. It is sometimes subconscious. It is not at the front of your thoughts but you have a 'feeling' about this thing.

Example 1: *He seemed nice enough but something at the back of my mind told me to not trust him.*

Example 2: *Even when I agreed to marry him, at the back of my mind I was thinking 'No don't do it, don't say yes'.*

To ferry someone around: this means to drive someone from place to place like a taxi service. This is usually used when talking about driving kids to school etc. It has a feeling that you don't really want to be driving this person everywhere.

Example: *I seem to spend half my life ferrying my son from one birthday party to another nowadays.*

In stark contrast to: 100% different to…. For Example, '*Bill, in stark contrast to his brother John, is very nice*' means that John is not nice at all.

Example: *In stark contrast to London, the surrounding areas are actually quite clean.*

To get under someone's feet: to get in the way. To obstruct someone by accident. This is usually used to describe when children are playing in the house and getting in the way of their parents doing things such as housework etc.

Example: *It's nice having the children home during the holidays but they tend to get under my feet. which makes doing things take twice as long.*

To make oneself scarce: this is a polite way to say 'go away'. To not bother someone and go somewhere else. Again this is often used in relation to children.

Example: *I have to clean the house so why don't you make yourself scarce for a few hours so I can just get on with it.*

Part Two

I asked a friend of mine who has kids what was going on? Was it my imagination or did kids actually not play outside any more. She told me that there had been a big change due to a lot of reasons. In some cases it was just parents wrapping their kids up in cotton wool and being overly protective. Also it was that, while in our day we didn't really have personal computers, now they are 10 a penny and almost every child has a games console. So lots of kids stayed inside playing computer games. I asked her what she felt about this development, and she said that even if she did send her kids out to play, they would stick out like a sore thumb because there wouldn't be any other kids out there. She told me that kids of 10 and above still went to the park but even that was happening less and less.

Phrases:

To wrap someone up in cotton wool: to be over protective of someone. This is a negative term and sounds like you are 'protecting' someone from reality and that it will probably have bad consequences.

Example: *They wrap that kid up in cotton wool, I think that she is going to struggle when she goes to school and has to deal with problems on her own.*

In (my etc) day: this can either mean 'when I was younger' or 'when I was there (working at a certain place etc)'.

Example 1: *There is a housing estate there now, but in my day it was all just fields.*

Example 2: *I heard that the company I used to work for has gone bust because of the bad economy. It's weird because in my day it was very successful, I never would have imagined that they would go bankrupt.*

10 a penny: a very common item.

Example: *In Japan, you hardly ever see dogs, but if you go to England they're ten a penny.*

To stick out like a sore thumb: to stand out. To be conspicuous. To be obvious.

Example: *When I was at school I used to stick out like a sore thumb because I was about 15cm taller than everyone else in my class.*

PART THREE

Now I'd be the first to admit that I have a tendency to look at the past through rose tinted glasses but I do think that it's a shame that kids don't play outside like they used to. When I was a kid I was out every day until it got dark. Sometimes of course I was up to no good but mostly I was just out messing around with my friends. Was it safer back then? I don't know, but I think that I learnt how to stand on my own two feet by dealing with problems and not avoiding them. Each to their own but I'd rather be outside in the park that staring at a games console any day of the week.

Phrases:

(I/she etc would be) the first to admit (that): this is used when you want to acknowledge something about your character before you make a certain point. For example if you were naughty at school when you were younger but (now as an adult) you want to say that some child is too naughty you would say *"I'd be the first to admit that I was bit naughty at school, but his behavior is completely unacceptable"*.

Example: *I'd be the first to admit that I like alcohol but to call me an alcoholic is ridiculous.*

To see things through rose tinted glasses: this is when you have an unrealistically good view of things. You see things as you wish they were and not as they were. It's often used about the past.

Example: My sister sees our father through rose tinted glasses, but actually when we were growing up he was way too strict.

To stand on one's own two feet: to be able to look after yourself. To have some independence.

Example: *My mother was always at work so I had to learn to stand on my own two feet from an early age.*

Each to their own: this basically means that it's up to the individual. Everyone has the right to their own choice or opinion. It is generally used when you don't agree with or understand their choice but you understand that it has nothing to do with you.

Example: *I don't understand why anyone would want to get a tattoo, but each to their own I guess.*

Any day of the week: this is used to express preferences. It means that you would 100% prefer this option over the other. It is often used as "I would prefer A over B any day of the week".

Example 1: *Some people love the heat but I'd choose a cold climate any day of the week.*

Example 2: *I'd take pasta over rice any day of the week.*

Jargon Buster

Part One

If there is one thing that really gets under my skin , it's 'buzz words'. These are popular phrases that are used in certain industries or fields. They are like jargon but are often in wider use. I can't begin to describe just how much I hate these words, if someone uses one of them in front of me it just puts me on edge. The ones I think I hate the most are the business type ones that have been becoming fashionable recently. For example 'Thinking outside the Box', this basically means to try to look at things at a different angle or to tackle something in an original or unusual way. Now of course there is nothing wrong with this phrase it's just that it's been completely overused. Also people even use it for things that are quite normal and are certainly *inside* the box. It seems that it has become a catch-all phrase when people want to say that they or their product is special even if it is as clear as day that it is not special at all.

Phrases:

To gets under one's skin: to (really) annoy you. This has the feeling of very subtly affecting someone in a bad way.

Example: *I don't know what it is about him, but he just really gets under my skin.*

To put one on edge: to make you feel uncomfortable. To make you feel tense.

Example1 : *Even if they haven't done anything wrong that teacher has a tendency to put his students on edge.*

Example 2: *Ever since I lost my job, I've been feeling really on edge.*

To think outside the box: to think about an issue/problem in a fresh/original way. To have a original way of thinking about things.

Example: *We need to stop employing yes-men and start getting people who can really think outside of the box.*

A catch-all phrase: a phrase or title that covers a large group of subjects. For example, 'Maths' covers (is a catch-all phrase for) the smaller areas of algebra and arithmetic.

Example: *The word 'Dance Music' is actually a catch-all phrase for lots of different types of music.*

To be clear as day: to be obvious.

Example: *Even though he denied it, it was clear as day that he was guilty. I mean there was video footage of him committing the crime.*

Part Two

The next type of 'buzz word' that I can't bare are the ones connected to buying a house. About 10 years ago there were suddenly loads of TV programmes about buying houses. It was like a disease that swept across the country. Everyone was obsessed with property and of course that went hand in hand with all of these TV programmes appearing everywhere. The presenters on these shows were nine times out of ten totally brain-dead and just repeated the same buzz words over and over again. One of the phrases was 'Wow Factor' which means a point or aspect (of the house) that really impresses you. The other phrase they always used was 'To Tick All of the Boxes'. This is when something (like a house) has everything you want/need and that it meets your expectations. Now I'm sure you're saying "if you hate these buzzwords so much why not just turn the TV off?" But the thing is that these words have made their way into everyday language now so there's no escaping them.

Phrases:

(I) can't bare (something): this means the same thing as 'I can't stand'. It means that you really don't like something. That you don't have any patience for something.

Example: *I can't bare it when children whine.*

To go hand in hand (with): together. This means that two things occur at the same time.

Example: *Politics and lying tend to go hand in hand.*

Nine times out of ten: usually. This can be used to emphasize the one time this thing didn't happen.

Example 1: *Nine times out of ten he can score a goal from that distance.*

Example 2: *Nine times out of ten he can score a goal from that distance, but this time he missed.*

Wow factor: something that impresses you about a house/product.

Example: *This house has a large garden and a swimming pool, it really has a wow factor.*

To tick all of the boxes: to fulfill all of your wishes for a certain thing.

Example: *This house has private parking and is close to a lot of good schools, it really ticks all of the boxes.*

Part Three

To wrap this chapter up I thought that I'd just list a few really awful ones and then let you know their meaning. As I said I don't know exactly what it is that bothers me about these buzz words/phrases, they just don't sit well with me.

One) **Blue sky thinking:** this is similar in meaning to 'think outside the box' and means thinking without limiting oneself. This one is often used in business.

Example: *We are getting nowhere using our usual marketing strategies, what we need now is some blue sky thinking.*

Two) **Singing from the same song sheet:** this one doesn't bother me too much but I know that a lot of people hate it. It means to have the same view/opinion on something as someone else.

Example: *Well it seems that we are all singing from the same song sheet so let's go ahead with the proposals.*

Three) **A game changer:** this refers to something that changes a whole industry or situation. So you could say that the IPhone was a game changer because it completely revolutionized that field. This again seems to be very over-used, and people sometime use it to refer to things that are definitely **not** game-changers!

Example: *The electric car is a real game changer.*

Four) **To hit the ground running:** this is often used in business and means to start doing something at full speed. To not slowly ease into something but to go completely into doing something.

Example: *We are working to a strict deadline so with this project we will have to hit the ground running.*

Other Phrases:

To wrap something up: to bring something to a close. To conclude something. It is often used in connection with projects, meetings etc.

Example: *Ok we have covered all of the items on the agenda so let's wrap this meeting up.*

(When Something) doesn't sit well with one: this is when you feel uncomfortable with a certain situation or thing. You disagree or are not happy with something.

Example: *Even though my boss was always nice to me it didn't sit well with me how he mistreated the other employees, so I eventually quit.*

Death of the Job. Birth of Opportunity

Part One

Contrary to what the newspapers or the government says, Britain is in a recession. Of course they do their utmost to convince everyone otherwise, but if you ask the man on the street he will tell you that his life has been financially a lot more difficult recently. Literally everyone I know has had to tighten their belts. A lot of my friends have been made redundant or have had their wages frozen. This is not really the place to discuss the cause of the recession, but the results in my opinion have been both good and bad. The bad are obvious, people have less money and continue to suffer even though they are not the ones to blame. I could fill this whole book with the bad effects of the recession but I'm a glass half full person so I prefer to concentrate on the positives.

Phrases:

Contrary to (popular opinion/what someone said): this means that even though someone/most people said/think(s) this, the truth is actually quite different.

Example: *Contrary to what most people think, the line 'play it again Sam' does not appear in the film Casablanca.*

To do one's utmost: this means to do everything you can to achieve something.

Example: *The police will do their utmost to find the runaways.*

The man on the street: this is used to describe an average/normal person. It's used to describe what 'most people' think/feel/experience and not just, for example rich people.

Example: *I don't think the man on the street has any idea who the head of the BBC is.*

To tighten one's belt: to make savings. To cut back on spending.

Example: *Since I lost my job, I've had to really tighten my belt.*

To have one's wages frozen: to stop getting pay rises. Some jobs get increases in line with inflation so if wages are frozen this means these people are getting poorer and poorer.

Example: *The council has completely run out of money so they have had to freeze their employee's wages.*

A glass half full (person): this means that you are optimistic. It refers to a glass of water that can be viewed as half empty (pessimistic) or as half full (optimistic).

Example: *Look at it as if the glass is half full, you may have lost your job, but at least you don't have to work with your awful boss any more.*

Part Two

What's positive about being in a recession? You'd have to be blind not to notice that inflation is sky high and that the standard or living for most people is dropping, so how can I say that there are positives? Well in my opinion I think that things are getting smaller and that rather than huge companies controlling everything, more and more individuals are striking out on their own and starting small companies. Before, people tended to just work for a company for their whole lives but now there is no such thing as a job for life. Actually in many areas there is no such thing as a job! For some people this has resulted in them just being unemployed and in a terrible situation. Others however have turned their bad luck to their advantage.

Phrases:

Sky high: this means very high. It is often used to describe prices.

Example: *The price of London property has gone sky high over the last 10 years.*

Standard of living: this describes the quality of someone's life. It usually refers to the financial state of someone's life. So if you have enough money to live on, clean water and sanitation then you have a good 'standard of living'.

Example: *On the whole the western standard of living is declining while in the east it is rising.*

To strike out on one's own: this is when you leave a team/company etc and start doing things on your own.

Example: *I left the family business and struck out on my own.*

No such thing: this thing doesn't exist.

Example: *There's no such thing as 'impossible'.*

To turn something to one's advantage: to take a situation that may not be favorable for you and to use it for your own benefit.

Example: *He turned his disability to his advantage and started a tour company especially for people with the same condition as him.*

PART THREE

I heard once that the Chinese word for *danger* is the same as their word for *opportunity*. I actually don't think that is a correct translation but it <u>illustrates my point</u> well. I heard recently about a woman who lost her job and had absolutely no idea how she was going to get another one. In order to save money she spent half of her days searching around for the best deals. Soon her friends and family started to follow her advice on where to get the best bargains. After a while <u>word spread</u> and complete strangers contacted her to get the <u>low down</u> on where the cheapest deals were locally. A bit later she started a website and let local businesses advertise on it. The website really <u>caught on</u> and ended up being an absolute <u>gold mine</u>. Now this woman is literally <u>rolling in it</u>.

Phrases:

To illustrate one's point: an example that is good for making a certain point .

Example: *The fact that that young men have the most car accidents illustrates my point that tests should be stricter for that group of people.*

Word spread: when people hear about something. When news of something is passed on naturally by friends etc.

To spread the word: this is similar to the above but is when someone actively spreads the news.

Example 1: *Word spread pretty quickly about the factory closing, within an hour the place was surrounded by angry employees.*

Example2 : *We are going to have a surprise party for Julie, could you spread the word amongst all of her friends please.*

To get the low down: this phrase could be considered to be slang, but it is in very wide use. It means to get all of the information about something. It sometimes relates to secret information.

Example: *I love that website, it really gives you the low down on what is actually happening in the finance world and not just what the newspapers report on.*

(For something) to catch on: this means when something becomes popular.

Example: *CDs were not that popular at first but after people realized how useful they were they soon caught on.*

Note: Be careful when using this phrase because if it is used about *someone* and not *something* then the meaning is 100% different. It then means that the person has realized something or discovered a secret etc. For Example: *John caught on to the fact that his wife was cheating on him.* This means that John discovered/realized that his wife was cheating.

A gold mine: a very profitable project/venture etc.

Example: *It's hard work, but restoring classic cars is an absolute gold mine nowadays.*

To be rolling in it: to be very rich. It refers to rolling in money.

Example: *I heard that her parents are absolutely rolling in it, so she will inherit it all at one point.*

The Wind up Merchant*

Part One

I think there's someone in everyone's life who we could basically do without. In my case it's a guy called Henry. Henry is a friend of my friend Joe. Joe's an excellent friend and I really enjoy hanging out with him. But for some reason he became friends with Henry and now they are always together. It's got to the point where if you invite Joe out, rain or shine Henry will definitely be there. Now the thing about Henry is that he seems ok but under the politeness he's basically a piece of work. He is what I would describe as passive aggressive, there's always two meanings to everything he says. The thing that really bothers me is that he loves to wind people up. So he finds something that bothers you and then just tries to push your buttons. Now after a while of this nonsense I decided to put an end to it once and for all.

*A 'wind up merchant' is someone who likes to wind other people up.

Phrases:

To do without (something): this means that you would rather not have this thing/person/situation in your life.

Example: *I have enough stress at work, I can do without having it at home as well.*

Rain or shine: this thing will happen any time and under any conditions.

Example: *I want you to know that you can come to me rain or shine if you have any problems.*

A piece of work: a very nasty person.

Example: *She was awful to him when we were growing up, she was a real piece of work.*

Passive aggressive: this describes someone who pretends to be nice but is actually aggressive. It is not connected with physical violence but more with psychological aggression. They sometimes say things as a 'joke' but they actually *want* to offend you or to hurt your feelings.

Example: *My boss is so passive aggressive, he says very nasty things and then pretends that he is saying them to 'help' me.*

To wind someone up: to slowly annoy someone (usually) on purpose. To say things that will (usually) intentionally annoy/irritate someone.

Example 1: *It really winds me up the way she always refuses to say sorry even if she knows that she is wrong.*

Example 2: *He tries to wind me up by talking about my ex-husband.*

To push someone's buttons: to find the points that annoy/irritate someone and then intentionally say/do things to cause the person to get annoyed.

Example: *After an argument he always pretends to be innocent, but he always intentionally tries to push my buttons.*

Once and for all: this is used to say that this is the final time. This will not happen again. It's often used in negative situations.

Example: *I have tried to fire him a few times but I don't because I just feel sorry for him. However, this time I'll do it once and for all.*

Part Two

The first thing I tried was just to ignore him. I thought that he would just get bored and leave me alone, but it completely <u>backfired</u> and it just made him even worse. Then I tried getting angry with him but he just pretended that there was no problem and that I should just relax. I couldn't get him to leave me alone <u>for love nor money</u> so eventually I decided that there was <u>only one thing for it</u>. I'd have to avoid seeing Joe so I wouldn't have to be around Henry any more. I felt bad about avoiding Joe but to be honest my dislike for Henry was so strong that I felt that it was worth it. After a while I started to relax and just sort of forgot about Henry. Then one Monday I turned up for work and couldn't believe my eyes; Henry was sitting at the desk next to mine.

Phrases:

For something to backfire: when something doesn't go as you planned it. The plan goes wrong. This is always used in a negative way.

Example: *I was planning on just speaking to my boyfriend about a few of his bad habits, but it backfired and we ended up having a huge argument and breaking up.*

(One wouldn't do this thing) for love nor money: this means that there is no way that you would do this thing.

Example: *After what he said to me I wouldn't forgive him for love nor money.*

There's only one thing for it: this is used when you feel that there is no alternative course of action.

Example: *I just can't find a job where I live so there's only one thing for it, I'll have to move to London.*

Part Three

My <u>jaw literally dropped to the floor</u>. My <u>mind began to race</u>. What was he doing there? What did he want? How could I avoid him? I quickly <u>made my way to</u> my boss's office and asked him what Henry was doing there. He told me that Henry was there for a job interview. When he saw the look on my face he asked what I thought of Henry. This completely <u>put me on the spot,</u> because even though I couldn't stand Henry I didn't want to interfere with his chances of getting a job. It was a complete moral dilemma; on the one hand I could tell the truth and my boss would never employ him, and on the other I could just <u>keep it to myself</u> and there would be a chance that Henry would become my new work colleague.

<u>Phrases:</u>

When one's jaw drops: this means that you are very shocked. You can use this as "my jaw dropped to the floor" which emphasizes that you were *really* shocked.

Example: *I thought she was still in prison so when I saw her on the bus talking to her friend, my jaw dropped.*

When one's mind races: this means that you start to panic and think about lots of different things in a disorderly way.

Example: *When I accused him of lying I could see that his mind was racing trying to think of an excuse.*

To make one's way to (somewhere): to go somewhere. This is sometimes used to emphasize *the journey*.

Example: *I am going to take a flight to Italy and then make my way back to England by train, stopping off at various places as I go.*

To put someone on the spot: to suddenly ask someone a question that they don't want to answer. To suddenly make someone feel uncomfortable about something. This is used when it's done both on purpose and unknowingly.

Example: *He really put me on the spot when he asked me if I knew if his wife had been cheating on him.*

To keep something to one's self: to not tell other people something. To keep a secret.

Example: *He won the lottery but he decided to keep it to himself because he was worried that people would begin to treat him differently.*

Part Four

For a second I was completely frozen and had no idea what to do. Then <u>against my better judgment</u> I decided to not say anything. I mean if I <u>let the cat out of the bag</u> I wouldn't have to put up with him* but I would have felt incredibly guilty. I heard later that day that Henry had actually got the job and to <u>add insult to injury</u> he would be working on the same team as me. For the next few weeks he was as <u>good as gold</u> and I <u>didn't hear a peep out of</u> him. This was mainly because I was training him so he needed my help. After a few months though, he had settled in and it wasn't long until he was <u>back to his old tricks again</u>.

*Wouldn't have to tolerate him.

<u>Phrases:</u>

Against one's better judgment: even though you have doubts you decide to do something that will benefit the other person. Even though you have doubts you decide to do this thing.

Example: *Against my better judgment I decided to not fire him and instead give him a second chance.*

To let the cat out of the bag: to tell a secret. To tell someone something that you shouldn't have.

Example: *It was supposed to be a secret but of course my sister let the cat out of the bag. She never thinks before she speaks.*

To add insult to injury: this is used when one bad thing happens and then another bad thing gets added to it.

Example: *After the divorce my wife got the house, and to add insult to injury I had to pay her monthly living expenses even though she has a better job than me.*

To be good as gold: to be well behaved. This is sometimes used about children.

Example: *The babysitter said that Timmy was as good as gold.*

To not hear a peep from/out of someone: when someone doesn't speak or make noise. To not hear from someone.

Example1: *He was so tired that I didn't hear a peep from him on the whole 2 hour journey.*

Example 2: *I saw him about a month ago but I haven't heard a peep out of him since.*

To be back to one's old tricks again: this refers to someone whose behavior was bad, then it improved, and now it has become bad again. They have returned to doing bad/naughty things.

Example: *The company was out of the news after they lost the law suit against them, but I heard that they are up to their old tricks again. So I wouldn't be surprised if they get sued again.*

Part Five

I talked to a few friends about what I should do about dealing with Henry's constant passive aggressive attitude. Most just said that I should try <u>to turn the other cheek</u> and ignore him. Others said that I should try to <u>get back at</u> him in some way, but I didn't want to <u>go down to his level</u>. One of my friends however, suggested that every time Henry said something that I didn't like, I should react in the exact opposite way that he was hoping for. So if he annoyed me I should laugh and if he was rude I should thank him for his help. I decided to give it a try. It was amazing, within about 2 weeks he completely gave up trying to wind me up and just left me alone. Unfortunately he chose someone else to <u>pick on</u>, and that person was not as patient as me. They went straight to the boss and made an official complaint. A few other people also made complaints and he was fired. I think this proves that <u>what goes around comes around</u>.

Phrases:

To turn the other cheek: this phrase refers to when you don't get angry at something. When you forgive someone for something. When you don't react when someone does something bad to you.

Example: *Usually I would just turn the other cheek, but I was so angry I started screaming at him.*

To get back at someone: to take revenge on someone/something. This usually means that someone does something bad to you so you do something bad to them. This is usually used for not very serious things.

Example: *She told my boss that I was late, so I got back at her by telling him that she has been taking 2 hour lunch breaks.*

To go down to someone's level: this means when someone does something bad to you, instead of ignoring it, you do something bad to them. This phrase implies that it is better to not do anything bad to the other person because then at least you have not done anything wrong yourself. If you do something bad as well, then you have 'dirtied' yourself in a way.

Example: *When he cheated on me I was going to do the same but I didn't want to go down to his level. Instead I just filed for divorce.*

To pick on someone: to bully someone. To be nasty to someone for no reason. This can be both mental and physical.

Example: *My older sister used to pick on me when we were kids. I think that is why we are not friends now.*

What goes around comes around: this means that if you do something bad, bad things will happen to you. Also if you do something good, good things will happen to you.

Example: *It's true what they say, what goes around comes around, because I volunteered at a charity and they gave me a job.*

INTERNET DATING

PART ONE

I am lucky enough to have a job that I absolutely love, however it is pretty demanding and I don't really have much time for a social life. Of course I have friends but for the past few years I haven't had a boyfriend. All of my friends are in relationships and I've started to feel like <u>the odd one out</u>. I suppose I could go out of my way to meet people, but I'm just so <u>rushed off my feet at work</u> that I don't have the energy. Usually things like blind dates and that kind of thing are <u>not my cup of tea</u> but '<u>needs must</u>', so I thought that I'd <u>give</u> internet dating <u>a go</u>.

Phrases:

To be the odd one out: the one person or thing that is different from the others. For example if all of your friends are men and you are a woman, then you would be the odd one out.

Example: *All of my family are teachers. So I'm the odd one out, as I'm a doctor.*

To be rushed off one's feet: to be very busy.

Example: *Christmas is a busy time of the year for most shops so the employees are usually rushed off their feet.*

Not one's cup of tea: you don't really like this sort of thing. This phrase is more common in British English.

Example: *Science fiction is not most women's cup of tea, but I like it.*

Needs must: it is necessary to do this thing. Circumstances have forced you to do this thing.

Example: *I didn't want to get an evening job, but as I don't have enough to live on; needs must.*

To give (something) a go/try: this means 'to try something to see if you like it'.

Example: *I thought that I would give cooking classes a go.*

PART TWO

I find talking about myself difficult <u>at the best of times</u>, so writing an online dating profile was going to be next to impossible. I sat down a few times to do it but could never get it done. I decided that it would require some <u>Dutch courage</u> so poured myself a nice big glass of wine and forced myself to write the profile. Most people when they are writing these things are <u>economical with the truth</u>, but my problem is that I am too honest. I read through the finished profile and I had to admit it didn't make me sound that appealing. The next thing that I had to do was to choose a photo. I know <u>you shouldn't judge a book by its cover</u> but everybody does so I tried to choose one where I looked at least <u>halfway decent</u>. In the end I was pretty satisfied with my profile even if was a little boring. It had taken me almost 5 hours to write but I eventually was ready to hit the 'publish' button. If I did this, <u>there would be no going back</u>; my profile would be there for the whole world to see. I held my breath and hit publish.

<u>Phrases:</u>

At the best of times: this phrase means that even under good conditions this thing is not great, so under bad conditions it's really bad.

Example: *Even at the best of times I get sea sick so if there is a storm (while I'm on a boat) then I feel really really sick.*

Dutch courage: to drink alcohol in order to feel brave about something.

Example: *I hate visiting my father in law so I find I need a bit of Dutch courage to make the experience manageable.*

To be economical with the truth: to lie a little bit. This has the feeling of not being a serious lie but just not exactly telling the truth. To exaggerate.

Example: *When applying for a job most people are a bit economical with the truth. But if you tell a real lie then you could end up getting into real trouble.*

You shouldn't judge a book by its cover: you shouldn't judge a person or situation just by appearances.

Example: *I know that you shouldn't judge a book by its cover but because he has a big scar on his face he does look a bit scary.*

To be halfway decent: to be quite good. To be ok. To be acceptable for what you need.

Example: *Do you know of any halfway decent hotels in this area?*

There is no going back: this means that you have committed to something and you can no longer decide to not do it.

Example: *I have handed in my notice at work so there's no turning back now. So next month I will have to get a new job.*

PART THREE

The next morning I woke up with butterflies in my stomach. I don't know why I was so nervous. Anyway I checked my email but no one had replied to my profile yet. Even though it was still early days I was a little disappointed. For the next few days I didn't get any response, and then just as I was about to close the profile down, I received an email. It was from someone called Tim who said that he had seen my profile and that he would really like to meet me. I checked out his profile and couldn't believe my luck; not only was he rich but he was gorgeous too. It was almost as if he was too good to be true. I really thought that I'd hit the jackpot; I mean he seemed so nice. We started contacting each other by email and soon we arranged to meet. I could hardly wait for our date. Unfortunately just a few hours before we were supposed to meet I received a phone call saying that something had come up and that we would have to take a rain check.

Phrases:

To have butterflies in one's stomach: to feel nervous about something.

Example: *Even though I have acted on stage for years, I still get butterflies in my stomach before every performance.*

It's early days: it is still early in a project/relationship etc.

Example: *The company hasn't made any money yet, but it's early days so we should make some profit once we have become more established.*

To check something out: to investigate something. To look at something in more detail.

Example: *I would like to move to France but I need to go there first to check out the work situation.*

I couldn't believe my luck: this is used when you feel that you have been really lucky.

Example: *I couldn't believe my luck when I realized that my land is actually twice as valuable as I first thought.*

To be too good to be true: this is used when you think that something is so good that there must be/could be a hidden problem.

Example: *That job just sounds too good to be true. Are you sure you know everything about it?*

To hit the jackpot: to win lots of money. To be lucky and receive a very good thing.

Example: *He hit the jackpot with that job. Both the money and the conditions are great.*

(I s/he etc) can hardly wait: you are very impatient for something to happen.

Example: *I can hardly wait for my birthday. Finally I will be able to take driving lessons.*

Something has come up: this is when something occurs that will delay something else. For example if you are at work and were going to go home 'when something came up'. This means that something that you had to deal with occurred and you were delayed returning home.

Example: *I was supposed to go to my mother's after work but something came up so I couldn't go.*

To take a rain check: to postpone doing something until a later date.

Example: *I'm sorry that I can't come this weekend but maybe we can take a rain check?*

Part Four

Even though we didn't meet up, we emailed and spoke other over the phone. He seemed really nice and was very flirty but whenever I suggested that we should meet, he'd just make an excuse or back out at the last minute. This happened a few times and I started <u>to smell a rat</u>. I told my friends about it and they agreed that there was <u>something fishy about</u> the whole thing and that I should just <u>call it quits</u>. I <u>didn't have the heart to</u> say anything on the phone so I just emailed him and said that I was very busy at work and wouldn't be able to contact him for a while. I think he <u>got the message</u> because he stopped calling and I never heard from him again.

<u>Phrases:</u>

To smell a rat: to suspect that something is not right. To suspect dishonesty of some sort.

Example: *The policeman smelt a rat when the woman wouldn't let him see what was inside her bag. It turned out that she had had just stolen it of off someone else.*

There's something fishy about (something): this means there is something not quite right about something.

Example: *There is something fishy about that couple. They never seem to work but they always have money.*

To call it quits: to put an end to something. This has the feeling of ending something before its natural conclusion.

Example: *After a few years of an unhappy marriage, me and my wife decided to just call it quits.*

(I, s/he etc) didn't have the heart to (do something): this means that you were intending to do something a bit unpleasant to someone but in the end you felt too bad and didn't do it.

Example: *I wanted to fire him immediately but as he has kids I didn't have the heart, so I gave him an extra 2 months to find a new job.*

To get the message: this is sometimes used when you don't tell someone something directly but your actions make it clear what you mean. Other times it is used when you did say it directly and they understood very clearly.

Example 1: *I didn't know how to tell him that I wanted him to move out of my house but I think he got the message because he told me that he would be moving next week.*

Example 2: *I told him that if he ever comes here again that I'd call the police. So I think that he got the message.*

Part Five

Anyway I sort of just <u>moved on</u> and forgot about the whole thing. Then one day I saw this documentary about this guy who met women online and then tried to <u>cheat them out of money</u>. They showed a photo and of course it was Tim, the guy that I'd met online. Apparently he'd done it to loads of women and had stolen thousands and thousands of pounds. Also it said that the photo that he'd used wasn't even him! He was in fact only 18 and he still lived with his mother. So <u>far from</u> being rich and successful he was just this strange young man you stole money from people. It goes to show that it is impossible to tell on the internet as people can pretend to be anybody they want to be. I really feel as though I <u>dodged a bullet</u> and will go back to the more traditional ways of meeting people.

Phrases:

To move on: to stop concerning yourself with a certain problem and to try to move past it and continue on with your life.

Example: *After my divorce, I just had to move on with my life.*

To cheat (someone) out of money: this means to steal. But it has the feeling that the money was stolen by deceiving someone rather than just taking it.

Example: *Jill's step mother cheated her out of her inheritance after her father died.*

Far from…..: this means that the situation/person is very different from previously stated. So if you are 'far from rich' then that means that you are poor.

Example: *Far from being dangerous, England is actually a very safe country.*

To dodge a bullet: this means that even though it didn't feel like it at the time, you actually avoided a bad situation.

Example: *Even though I was upset when I didn't get the job, it turns out that I dodged a bullet because I heard that the boss there is horrible and that the employees have to do unpaid over-time.*

THE FAMILY HOLIDAY

PART ONE

Last year my mother rang me and asked me if I wanted to go on a family holiday with her, my father and my sister. Sounds like fun right? Wrong! Actually I really enjoyed my childhood and always got on with my family really well, but for some reason we always had the worst family holidays. Anyway, I don't know why (perhaps it was because she <u>caught me off guard</u>) but I just "yes mum that sounds great, <u>count me in</u>". For the next few days after agreeing I tried to convince myself that it would be fun. But the more I remembered the old holidays the more it <u>sank in</u> just what a terrible idea this was. For one thing, my father always insists on driving to the destination as he is afraid of flying. So it always takes forever to get there. Also my mother is the worst back-seat driver* ever so my parents just end up arguing the whole journey. At least my sister would be there. Oh I forgot. My sister gets car sick so she would just be complaining the whole time! After a few days of thinking back I really regretted agreeing to go. I must have been <u>out of my mind.</u>

*A back seat driver is someone who is a passenger but constantly interferes with the driver and tells them what to do.

Phrases:

To catch one off guard: this means that you were not expecting something. This has the feeling that you are surprised by something and so are unprepared to deal with it properly. It also has the feeling that someone did something to you when you were vulnerable so you couldn't defend yourself.

Example: *She caught me off guard when she asked me if she would get the promotion. I wasn't prepared so I just admitted that there was no way she would get it.*

To count one in: this means 'yes I will participate'. It means that you are happy to join the activity.

Example: *Person 1) Do you want to go sailing this weekend? Person 2) Definitely, count me in.*

For something to sink in: to slowly realize the reality of a situation. This can be used for both positive and negative situations.

Example: *It took a few months for it to sink in after I'd won the lottery.*

To be out of one's mind: to be totally crazy. To not be thinking straight.

Example: *Anyone who does a bungee jump must be out of their mind.*

Part Two

I knew from the word go that this holiday was a bad idea. But every time I told my mum that it would be a nightmare she would just insist that we go. She said that it would be fun and that we would just take a relaxed drive to the South of France and then stay there for a few days and then head back. Relaxed? Chance would be a fine thing! Actually our problems started as soon as we had set off. My mother was reading the map but kept saying that she couldn't make head nor tail of it, so we soon got lost. It was hardly surprising because the map was 30 years out of date. My father is so tight fisted that he wouldn't buy a new up-to-date map even if his life depended on it. Anyway I eventually bought a new map and we managed to get back on the right road.

Phrases:

From the word go: from the very beginning.

Example: *I knew from the word go that I wanted to be a doctor.*

Chance would be a fine thing: this phrase means that the *thing* is very unlikely to happen.

Example: *They said that the weather would be good today. But as I live in England, chance would be a fine thing.*

(I s/he etc) couldn't make head nor tail of something: you couldn't understand something at all.

Example: *I couldn't make head nor tale of that film.*

To be up-to-date/ out of date: if something is *up to date* then it is the current version and will work fine. If it is *out of date* then it is not current and will not work anymore. For example if your car insurance is *up to date* then you are insured. If it is *out of date* and then something happens to your car, then you are not insured.

Example 1: *The government writes to me every year to make sure that my car registration details are still up to date.*

Example 2: *My computer software is out of date so I can't open the document properly.*

To be tight fisted: to never want to spend money, even if you have to. To not be generous with money.

Example: *My husband is so tight fisted. We have not been out for dinner in 10 years.*

(To not do something) even if one's life depended on it: this means that you would never under any circumstances do this thing.

Example: *I wouldn't forgive him even if my life depended on it.*

Part Three

The fact that we got lost as soon as we set off was a bit worrying but after that we made it to France <u>without a hitch</u>. I thought that I'd have to <u>eat my words</u> because it was turning out to be better than I expected. <u>No sooner had I</u> thought that perhaps it would be ok, things started to go wrong. First we had a puncture, then my sister was sick and we had to stop for a while. Then we lost the map and eventually got lost again. I decided that enough was enough and as a last resort* suggested that we find a nice hotel in that area and then just stay there. Much to my surprise everybody agreed. I think that everyone was fed up of driving and knew that we <u>would be better off</u> just <u>staying put</u>.

Phrases:

(It went etc) without a hitch: the event/process etc proceeded with absolutely no problems at all.

Example: *I was nervous about my wedding but the whole thing went without a hitch.*

To eat one's words: to say something negative and then later have to admit that you were wrong.

Example: *I used to always say bad things about her husband, but it actually seems like he's a pretty nice guy. It seems that I'll have to eat my words.*

No sooner had I…: this means the same as 'as soon as I had…' It has the feeling that you do or say one thing and then the opposite (or unexpected thing) occurs.

Example: *No sooner had I got my car serviced when it was stolen.*

Would be better off…: would be in a better position/situation if….

Example: *Being self employed is so tiring, sometimes I wonder if I'd be better off just working for a company.*

To stay put: to stay where you are. To not move around.

Example: *After I graduated I wanted to travel the world, but most of my friends just wanted to stay put.*

Part Four

We soon found a really nice hotel and decided to stay there for the whole holiday. Although it wasn't where we were planning to go initially, it was in a lovely area. Anyway we all agreed that it was miles better than being cooped up in a car for two days getting on each other's nerves. We had a great holiday and were all sad when it was over. My mother has tried to convince me that we should do it again, but I think I'll quit while I'm ahead!

Phrases:

To be miles better than (something else): to be a lot better than (something else).

Example: *I know a lot of people like to travel by plane, but I think boats are miles better because they are so much fun.*

To be cooped up (somewhere): this is when you are confined in a small space.

Example: *I hate being ill because I have to stay cooped up in my room all the time.*

To get on (someone's) nerves: to annoy someone.

Example: *That actor get's on my nerves. I think it's because I don't like his voice.*

To quit while one is ahead: to stop doing something when you are still in profit or in a good position. To quit while things are good and before they possibly go wrong.

Example: *She is very difficult to get on with, but after a few minutes of conversation she seemed to at least smile a little bit. So I decided to quit while I was ahead and make an excuse and leave.*

GOODBYE

Well you have reached the end of this book. I hope that you have enjoyed it and am sure that your English has improved a lot. I know that all of your hard work will <u>pay off</u> and you will be fluent in no time.

Also I'd like to <u>thank you from the bottom of my heart</u> for choosing this book.

Phrases:

For (something) to pay off: to gain the reward of lots of hard work.

Example: *He trained night and day, but all of his hard work paid off in the end when he won the competition.*

To thank (someone) from the bottom of one's heart: to be very thankful for something.

Example: *The actress thanked the director from the bottom of her heart for putting her in the film.*

Please be sure to visit my website for a free newsletter, listening downloads and information on my other books. Plus a lot more to help you reach your goal of English fluency.

www.englishfluencytoday.com

www.ingramcontent.com/pod-product-compliance
Lightning Source LLC
Chambersburg PA
CBHW051947290426
44110CB00015B/2140